WEAPON

THE FN FAL BATTLE RIFLE

BOB CASHNER

Series Editor Martin Pegler

First published in Great Britain in 2013 by Osprey Publishing,
Midland House, West Way, Botley, Oxford, OX2 0PH, UK
43-01 21st Street, Suite 220B, Long Island City, NY 11101
E-mail: info@ospreypublishing.com

Osprey Publishing is part of the Osprey Group

A CIP catalogue record for this book is available from the British
Library

Print ISBN: 978 1 78096 903 9
PDF ebook ISBN: 978 1 78096 904 6
ePub ebook ISBN: 978 1 78096 905 3

Index by Sandra Shotter
Typeset in Sabon and Univers
Battlescenes by Steve Noon
Originated by PDQ Media, Bungay, UK
Printed in China through Worldprint Ltd

13 14 15 16 17   10 9 8 7 6 5 4 3 2 1

Osprey Publishing is supporting the Woodland Trust, the UK's
leading woodland conservation charity, by funding the dedication
of trees.

www.ospreypublishing.com

Dedication
To my wife.

Acknowledgements
I would like to express my thanks to the many people who made
this project possible, including Colonel Paul Farrar, Ian Rhodes,
James Scott, David Miller, Steve Cone, Tom Moore, Steve Creamer,
and the whole gang at the FAL Files. As well, Nick Reynolds and
Tom Milner at Osprey deserve particular recognition for going
above and beyond their duties in publishing this work.

Imperial War Museum Collections

Many of the photos in this book come from the Imperial War
Museum's huge collections which cover all aspects of conflict
involving Britain and the Commonwealth since the start of
the twentieth century. These rich resources are available online
to search, browse and buy at www.iwmcollections.org.uk. In
addition to Collections Online, you can visit the Visitor Rooms
where you can explore over 8 million photographs, thousands
of hours of moving images, the largest sound archive of its
kind in the world, thousands of diaries and letters written by
people in wartime, and a huge reference library. To make an
appointment, call (020) 7416 5320, or e-mail mail@iwm.org.
uk.

Imperial War Museum www.iwm.org.uk

Editor's note

The editor would like to thank Neil Grant for kindly supplying
photographs for this book, and the staff and trustees of the
Small Arms School Corps museum, for invaluable access to
their collections.

For ease of comparison please refer to the following conversion
table:
1 mile = 1.6km
1yd = 0.9m
1ft = 0.3m
1in = 2.54cm/25.4mm
1lb = 0.45kg

Artist's note

Readers may care to note that the original paintings from which
the battlescenes in this book were prepared are available for
private sale. All reproduction copyright whatsoever is retained
by the Publishers. All enquiries should be addressed to:

www.steve-noon.co.uk

The Publishers regret that they can enter into no correspondence
upon this matter.

Cover images are courtesy of Rock Island Auction Company
(top) and US DoD (bottom).

CONTENTS

INTRODUCTION

World War II showed that the age of the manually operated bolt-action or single-shot military rifle had come to an end. Self-loading rifles – weapons that reloaded themselves automatically with every pull of the trigger – were the future. Yet while the United States' M1 Garand rifle – the world's first standard-issue self-loading rifle – was a milestone and well liked by all who used it, its use of a limited eight-round en bloc clip rather than a detachable box magazine of higher capacity would lead to its demise. (The en bloc clip required the user to push a clip of eight rounds as a single unit down into a fixed magazine.) A new post-war self-loading rifle was obviously needed. But what form would it take?

The German StG 44 *Sturmgewehr* (Assault Rifle) had made a great impression during the waning years of World War II. The StG 44 fired the 7.92×33mm *kurz* (short) round, an 'intermediate' type of ammunition, launching a 125-grain projectile at 701m/sec (2,300ft/sec). The power of this cartridge offered a perfect compromise between the weak and short-ranged pistol calibres used in submachine guns and the full-power, hard-kicking rifle cartridges.

The Soviet Union was quick to grasp the intermediate-cartridge concept. With massed conscripted armies often receiving only rudimentary training before being rushed into battle, marksmanship and live-fire practice were given short shrift. What was needed was a simple, reliable weapon that could be operated effectively by even the most hastily trained soldier.

The AK-47 (*Avtomat Kalashnikova* 47) was that weapon, and it became the quintessential assault rifle. Using the 7.62×39mm round, the AK-47 was an utterly reliable gas-operated firearm capable of taking severe abuse in the field and remaining functional. It was also easy to mass-produce. While the AK's short-lived immediate predecessor in Soviet service, the SKS, had an integral magazine that required reloading via ten-round stripper clips or chargers, the AK-47 had a 30-round detachable

box magazine. Its major claim to fame, however, was having a select-fire capability – the ability to fire either semi-automatic or full-automatic – with a cyclic rate of 600rds/min. Throughout its lifespan, the AK-47 was constantly modified and adapted, with the AKM being the most widely produced version. Tens of millions have been made all over the world for use by various armies, and it has become the favoured weapon of insurgents everywhere.

The West needed an answer to the AK-47. Even before the AK-47 appeared on the world scene, Western nations were studying the concept of an assault-type rifle, but it would be a long and twisting road to travel before they arrived at one. Political considerations trumped test performance in too many instances. While the Western nations involved arrived at various solutions, the results were technically main battle rifles rather than true assault rifles firing an intermediate cartridge.

One of the solutions – by sheer numbers the 'best' solution – was the FN FAL. The weapon originated with Belgium's famous Fabrique Nationale (FN) as the *Fusil Automatique Léger*, or Light Automatic Rifle, but it was almost universally known by its initials: FAL. To this day, many still refer to the FAL as an assault rifle. As we shall see shortly, it is not. Rather, correctly it is a main battle rifle, or MBR. It was indeed intended to be an assault rifle in its own right, but a variety of circumstances prevented it from becoming one.

As a main battle rifle, it was superb for its day, with many considering it the quintessential Cold War-era battle rifle. Perhaps it no longer seems so high-tech. It is an air-cooled, magazine-fed, gas-operated and (originally) select-fire rifle. Yet the FAL was rugged and reliable and offered greater range and accuracy than its Soviet- and Chinese-made assault-rifle opponents. It essentially did everything required by the men who carried it. Eventually, it would serve more than 90 different nations around the world and be given the nickname of 'The Right Arm of the Free World'.

The FN FAL was one of the most iconic rifles of the Cold War, in some ways the West's equivalent of the Kalashnikov assault rifle. Here, a FAL-armed Contra fighter stands guard at the edge of a base camp in Honduras, 1983, during the Nicaraguan Civil War. (Steven Clevenger/Getty Images)

DEVELOPMENT
The genesis of the FAL

THE WEST SEEKS AN ASSAULT RIFLE

A new calibre?

In the West, the utility and performance of smaller rifle calibres had been examined before 1945. Prior to World War I, Britain had been developing the .276in Enfield cartridge, which made it as far as troop trials. With war clouds gathering in Europe, however, it was the wrong time to attempt to switch to a new calibre and new weapons. In the 1930s, the Americans worked on the .276in Pederson, firing a 125-grain bullet at 823m/sec (2,700ft/sec). A Canadian-born American firearms designer named John Cantius Garand (1888–1974) had designed a then-revolutionary semi-automatic battle rifle, the T3E2, around the proposed new .276in cartridge and a ten-round clip. Pressure on US military budgets during the Depression era resulted in its quick demise, despite its performance. Yet Garand was able to redesign his rifle successfully to use the standard .30-calibre US cartridge in an eight-round clip, and it went on to be the pre-eminent self-loading rifle of World War II.

After 1945 the nations of the fledgling North Atlantic Treaty Organization (NATO), looking back on the endless variety of different ammunition types and weapons used during World War II, decided that a universal calibre amongst the member states was necessary. Once such a calibre was standardized, it was hoped that perhaps a universal infantry rifle could be adopted as well. The British again threw their efforts into truly innovative new intermediate cartridges: a .270in (6.8mm) round, firing a 130-grain bullet; and the .280in (7×43mm) round, firing a 140-grain bullet

at a muzzle velocity of 747m/sec (2,450ft/sec). Of the two, the latter was deemed the better prospect. Loaded with recently improved Winchester smokeless powder, it went on to achieve muzzle velocities of 792m/sec (2,600ft/sec). The heavier bullet also served as a sop towards the Americans and their insistence on larger calibres. The American military establishment clung to the belief that every American boy was a natural-born marksman who would need the ability to hit individual targets at long ranges. The Korean War would soon prove otherwise, for a variety of reasons.

The third and final version of the experimental cartridge was the .280/30. This cartridge case's base and rim were even given dimensions identical to those of the US .30-06 calibre, to make conversion of American weapons to the new calibre easier and also help ammunition manufacturers to switch over. It was hoped this would make the new round more acceptable to American politicians and military decision-makers.

The .280in was a true intermediate assault-rifle calibre, offering excellent performance out to 594m (650yd) – on a par with the heavier 7.62×51mm NATO round that was to be adopted instead, but with less weight, muzzle blast and considerably less recoil than the NATO round. Like the AK-47's 7.62×39mm round, the .280in could be better controlled than the 7.62×51mm round in full-automatic fire at close ranges in the assault, yet it far outranged and outperformed the Soviet round. It was also greatly superior in performance in terms of range and stopping power compared to the later 5.56×45mm NATO round. Indeed, to open-minded military officials, the .280in seemed to offer the best of both worlds.

Despite the enthusiastic support of military men in Britain, Canada and Belgium to adopt the .280in as the new universal NATO calibre, the US military balked. The stumbling block to several nations and the fledgling NATO alliance came down to one man, Colonel René Studler (1895–1980), chief of the US Small Arms Development Branch.

Colonel Studler's backing for the full-power T65 rifle cartridge resulted in the adoption of the 7.62mm NATO, and the United States ordering the M14. Photographed in Vietnam in 1965, these Marines are still armed with M14s, but already the intermediate-cartridge M16 was starting to replace the M14. (US Marine Corps)

After World War II and the great drawdown of the American military, the ambitious Colonel Studler saw his career plateau with no more great advances before his retirement. With the push for a standardization of calibre for NATO countries, Studler foresaw one last chance at a great coup. If he could develop the new NATO standard cartridge, it would probably mean a star on his shoulder. Furthermore, if he could develop an American rifle around the new calibre, which other NATO countries could be persuaded to adopt, he could perhaps crown his career as 'armourer to the Free World' and as a major player at NATO headquarters until his retirement.

Studler placed all his bets on the T65 cartridge, which would eventually become the 7.62×51mm NATO. The new Winchester ball propellants delivered the same performance as the old .30-06 with a considerably smaller amount of powder, enabling the cartridge case to be shortened significantly.

In no way could the T65 be considered to offer an intermediate or assault-rifle calibre, or even a great leap forward in cartridge design. It was still a full-power .30 round, essentially a .30-06 with a cartridge case 51mm long rather than 63mm. Since this small difference led to so much disagreement between NATO nations, some referred to it as 'the longest fifth of an inch in the world' (Rose 2008: 233). But the shorter T65 cartridge did enable rifles designed to fire it to have a shorter, and thus lighter, receiver than those employing the .30-06. Even so, the T65 was much too powerful for shoulder-fired full-automatic use and could not be built into a true assault rifle. It may have become an excellent round, but it was most certainly not intermediate. (As an indication of how profoundly those in American military circles misunderstood the assault rifle, for many years official US Army documents referred to the AK-47 as a 'submachine gun'.)

Colonel Studler also set his designers at Springfield Arsenal, Massachusetts, to create the 'perfect' weapon to fire his pet cartridge. It had to be able to replace and perform the roles of those weapons used at that time by the US military – the .30-06 M1 Garand rifle, the .30 M1 Carbine, the .45 Thompson and M3 submachine guns, and the .30-06 Browning Automatic Rifle – in one fell swoop. At the same time, the new weapon must reduce the infantryman's burden to less than 4kg (9lb). It would be possible to slim down the 4.3kg (9.5lb) Garand, but replacing the 10kg (22lb) BAR would be another story altogether. As the final hurdle, the new rifle had to be able to use 85 per cent of the existing M1 Garand's industrial tooling and equipment for production. All in all, it was a tall – and rather ridiculous – order.

On the other side of the Atlantic, the British had been working hard not only on the genuinely intermediate .280in round, but also on a revolutionary new infantry rifle, the EM-2, with which to use it. What made this rifle truly innovative was its 'bullpup' design. The breech mechanism and magazine were contained within the stock rather than in front of it; thus it could retain a normal-length barrel while still reducing overall length. The EM-2 came a great deal closer to the pie-in-the-sky requirements of Studler's new weapon than any of his own projects. As noted by the British Ministry of Defence (MoD) in 1950:

The general characteristics of the weapon are its versatility and its power of delivering either rapid single round [semi-automatic] fire or a volume of fire with the employment of a single man. The weapon can be fired as a self-loading rifle, a sub machine gun or (with the addition of a bipod) a light machine gun. Its effective range as a self-loading rifle is 500-yards. When fired from the bipod its effective range can be increased to 800-yards. With the addition of a grenade launcher, it can project a 1-¼ pound grenade to a maximum range of 250 yards. It can also be fitted with a bayonet. (British Army 1950: 1)

The EM-2 was an advanced British bullpup assault rifle, chambered for the intermediate .280 cartridge. It was never adopted, as the .280 round was rejected by NATO in favour of 7.62mm, and Britain instead adopted the L1A1 SLR. (Neil Grant)

No matter how well the .280in cartridge – or the weapons designed to shoot it – performed, the British project was doomed, as we shall see.

Enter the Belgians

The Belgians had also long been working on a new semi-automatic infantry rifle. Designers at Fabrique Nationale de Herstal in Liège began working on a gas-operated self-loading rifle in 1936, the same year the Americans adopted the M1 Garand rifle. Chief among the designers of the rifle was Dieudonné Joseph Saive (1889–1973), a Belgian native. Saive was an employee of Fabrique Nationale, where his ideas and skills attracted attention, and he eventually became chief design assistant to the legendary American firearms designer John Moses Browning (1855–1926).

When Browning died of a heart attack at his work bench, Saive took over the project his boss had been working on: a design for a self-loading pistol. After considerable development, including Saive's own staggered-row 13-round box magazine, which doubled cartridge capacity without making the grip too wide, the pistol was finally adopted by the Belgian Army in 1935 as the GP 35 ('GP' standing for Grand Puissance, or High Power) in 9mm Parabellum. It came to be known to the rest of the world as the Browning Hi-Power and is still in use today.

By the beginning of 1940, FN had developed the rifle design to the point where they were ready to manufacture and market it. The timing, of course, was disastrous, as the Nazi war machine overran the Low Countries that May. Saive and his design team managed to destroy all the design material for their new rifle and escape to Britain. Saive and his team offered their services to the British military. While officials were impressed, the fall

An early FN FAL with wooden furniture and a conical flash hider. (Neil Grant)

of France had left Britain all alone to resist the German war machine and much of the British Army's weaponry had been abandoned on the beaches of Dunkirk. It was certainly not the time to adopt a new rifle or, more importantly, to retool factories to manufacture it.

After Belgium's liberation, Saive went back to work on his original design. It was a slow process. Almost all of Europe had been devastated by the war, with cities and industries in ruins and millions dead or homeless. Saive's first post-war effort was the FN Modèle 1949, often known as the SAFN (*Saive Automatique, Fabrique Nationale*). The SAFN, made in various calibres, was a semi-automatic rifle with a ten-round detachable box magazine; it offered performance on a par with the M1 Garand. The SAFN was easily adapted to customer needs, and was manufactured in .30-06, 8×57mm, 7×57mm, 7.62×51mm NATO and 7.65×53mm calibres. The weapon was purchased by Argentina, Brazil, Colombia, the Congo, Egypt, Indonesia, Luxembourg and Venezuela. Belgium sent a battalion of well-trained crack troops as part of UN forces fighting in the Korean War, and the SAFN reportedly gave these soldiers yeoman service in harsh conditions.

While the SAFN was a good rifle, using the same gas operation and tilting-bolt mechanism later employed by the FAL, the timing was wrong once more. By the time the SAFN was introduced, the West was already attempting to leave behind the bolt-action and semi-automatic battle rifles and seeking an assault-type rifle. Perhaps the SAFN's most important contribution was providing sufficient sales to help Fabrique Nationale recover from Europe's wartime destruction and post-war financial ruin.

Even as the SAFN was being prepared for full production, Dieudonné Saive and Ernest Vervier had already produced a 1947 prototype of what would become the FAL, originally chambered for the German 7.92×33mm *kurz* (short) assault-rifle round. When introduced to the .280in British round, Fabrique Nationale's designers very much liked what they saw in the cartridge and further specimens of their new rifle were chambered for the British intermediate cartridge.

In either calibre, the FN weapon had great potential as a true assault rifle. The new FN prototype rifles came in three 'flavours': a 485mm (19.1in) barrel carbine version was intended for general infantry use; a 560mm (22.1in) barrel model with a bipod was intended to be a squad automatic weapon (SAW) or light machine gun (LMG); and a bullpup short rifle was most likely intended to compete with the British EM-2, were that project to take off. All three models offered a significant increase in infantry firepower along with reduced weight and length when compared to the full-size World War II-era Allied battle rifles of the day.

The potential of the bullpup design for compactness is obvious in the table below. While the FN short rifle (bullpup) has a barrel some 127mm (5in) longer than that of the relatively short and handy US M1 Carbine, the FN weapon was still shorter overall.

With a NATO standard round yet to be adopted, the British took examples of their EM-2 and of the FAL in .280in calibre to compete with the American entry, the T25, in the 1950 Light Rifle Trials. None of the rifles measured up to the tests; all of the weapons were essentially still prototypes, with refinements yet to be made. Of the contenders, however, the FN rifle made the best impression on the US Army's Infantry Board at Fort Benning, Georgia, with the adjudicators considering it to be the best of the bunch. They were also quite enthusiastic about the .280/30 round.

Low-ranking infantry officers, however, do not get to make such decisions as which rifle to equip fighting men with. Colonel Studler would

The heavy-barrelled FN FALO (*Fusil Automatique Lourd*) squad automatic weapon. (Neil Grant)

FN prototypes compared to conventional Western military rifles

	M1 Garand	No. 4 Mk 2 Lee-Enfield	M1 Carbine	FN Short Barrel	FN Long Barrel	FN Short Rifle (Bullpup)
Country	USA	UK	USA	Belgium	Belgium	Belgium
Calibre	.30-06 calibre	.303in	.30 calibre	7.92×33mm *kurz*	7.92×33mm *kurz*	7.92×33mm *kurz*
Barrel length	610mm (24in)	640mm (25.2in)	458mm (18in)	485mm (19.1in)	560mm (22.1in)	585mm (23in)
Overall length	1,106mm (43.5in)	1,128mm (44.4in)	904mm (35.6in)	985mm (38.8in)	1,060mm (41.7in)	860mm (33.9in)
Empty weight	4.3kg (9lb 8oz)	4.11kg (9lb)	2.36kg (5lb 3oz)	3.92kg (8lb 10oz)	4.05kg (8lb 15oz)	3.91kg (8lb 10oz)
Loaded weight	4.5kg (10lb)	4.36kg (9lb 10oz)	2.77kg (6lb 2oz) (15-round magazine); 2.99kg (6lb 10oz) (30-round magazine)	4.535kg (10lb)	4.665kg (10lb 5oz)	4.525kg (10lb)
Capacity	Eight-round en bloc clip	Ten-round magazine	15- or 30-round detachable box	20-round detachable box	20-round detachable box	20-round detachable box
Sights	183–1,097m (200–1,200yd)	91–1,189m (100–1,300yd)	137–229m (150–250yd)	100–600m (109–656yd)	100–600m (109–656yd)	100–600m (109–656yd)
Cyclic rate of fire	Semi-automatic only	Manual bolt	M1: semi-automatic only M2: 750–850rds/min	550rds/min	550rds/min	550rds/min

not back down from his pet project, the T65 cartridge. American insistence on the 7.62×51mm round sounded the death knell for the EM-2. Having been specifically designed around the .280in cartridge, it could not be reworked to take the heavier, more powerful .30-calibre load.

One British Army officer summed up their sincere efforts to advance the EM-2 and the .280-calibre thus: they had been 'Studlered'. A huge international row developed over the new standardized NATO cartridge. The British went so far as to officially adopt the EM-2 as the 'Rifle, Automatic, Calibre .280, No. 9 Mk 1', although it was never actually issued to troops. Eventually, political considerations prevailed and the Americans got their way, and the 7.62×51mm became NATO standard in 1954.

A new NATO cartridge

Now that the NATO cartridge was official, a new rifle had to be developed for it. Although they had also been enthusiastic about the .280in, the Belgians hedged their bets and worked to redesign the FAL to use the 7.62×51mm cartridge.

In 1953, the US Army conducted a new series of tests involving the 'FN Lightweight Cal. 30 Rifle' pitted against the American T44, both these weapons being in 7.62×51mm. Once more, the FN's performance

was sufficiently strong to prompt the Infantry Board to make two recommendations; as well as calling for a limited procurement of the FN rifle, they urged a halt to development of the T44. Once again, however, infantry officers did not get the final say in weapons procurement.

The next big showdown came in December 1953, when the rifles were sent to Fairbanks, Alaska, for the Arctic Winter Tests. While the FNs were boxed up at Fort Benning after the first trials and sent directly to Fairbanks, the T44s stopped off at Springfield Armory en route. For several weeks experts went over the rifles with a fine-tooth comb, testing and retesting them in the Armory's cold chamber, and making various hand-fitted individual modifications to ensure the weapons would perform well in the cold. Of course, the T44s beat the FNs handily in the Arctic Winter Tests.

Meanwhile, there had been an informal behind-the-scenes deal in which the Pentagon, the headquarters of the US Department of Defense, had promised Belgian representatives that the US Army would adopt the FAL as their new rifle if the Belgians in turn supported the American efforts to adopt the 7.62×51mm round. Once the new NATO round was adopted, however, the United States chose its own rifle design, the M14.

During the same period, Canada had gone along with the adoption of the T65 cartridge, but in 1954 had ordered 2,000 FALs from FN for troop trials and testing. Canada became the first country officially to adopt the FAL for military use, as the C1, in 1956. One by one, other nations would follow, until over 90 countries used the rifle. The United States would not be one of them. Colonel Studler, right before his own retirement in 1953, had set in motion the chain of events that would lead to the M14 rifle being officially adopted as America's new issue military rifle in 1957. While the Americans attempted to get other NATO nations to adopt it, they had few takers. The Nationalist Chinese in Taiwan, formerly Formosa, adopted it, but at that time they depended almost entirely upon American largesse to equip their military. The rest of the Free World was looking towards Belgium and the FAL.

Two British soldiers with L1A1s take part in Exercise *Barbican II* in the mountains of Cyprus during the 1960s. (IWM MH 33983)

'Inch' and 'Metric' patterns

There are two major 'types' of FAL: the so-called 'Inch' pattern and the 'Metric' pattern. When Britain adopted the FAL as the L1A1 SLR (Self-Loading Rifle), dimensions were converted to imperial measurements. For other nations outside the former Commonwealth, the original metric patterns remained standard. Most, but not all, parts are interchangeable between Inch and Metric FALs. For instance, the British SLR can use either Inch- or Metric-pattern magazines, but Metric FALs cannot use Inch-pattern magazines.

In addition to their different dimensions, the British and Commonwealth SLRs were all semi-automatic only, not even capable of being converted to full-automatic, at least not 'officially'. Other changes used in the Inch-pattern SLR included: the long flash hider with bayonet lug; a folding cocking handle; a folding rear sight; and an enlarged change lever/safety and magazine release, which are much easier to manipulate, especially when wearing gloves or mittens. The Metric FAL has seven adjustments to its gas block while the SLR has 11. Oddly enough, the British deleted the bolt hold-open device, which locks the bolt to the rear when the last round is fired from the magazine, a feature usually considered quite desirable.

INTO SERVICE

Canada

In the Canadian Army, as well as the militaries of the UK and other Commonwealth countries, the FAL had some very big shoes to fill. The .303in Lee-Enfield bolt-action rifle, in its various guises, was a long-used and beloved infantry weapon known for its sturdiness, reliability, power and accuracy. The latest version, still in use, was the No. 4 Mk I. Despite the sterling reputation of the Lee-Enfield, the Canadian military was more than happy with its acquisition of the FAL, with Colonel Bingham, Director of Infantry, noting:

> We have encountered no difficulty in the training of personnel to use this weapon. The design of the weapon lends itself to easy instruction due to the limited number of working parts. Recruits have no more difficulty understanding and operating this weapon than they did with the No 4. I feel the big feature of this Rifle is the improvement in marksmanship. The recruit of today becomes a better shot with less effort than in the days of the No 4. This factor greatly influences the soldier in his early training and gives him the required confidence in the Rifle. (Quoted in Stevens 1982: 107)

The Canadians adopted variants both of the FAL rifle and the FN FALO squad automatic weapon, their version of the latter being developed jointly with Australia. The heavy-barrelled C2, seen here, featured a novel bipod/handguard arrangement, the wood-shrouded legs of the bipod folding back to become the handguard. (Spec Vince E. Warner/DoD)

Like the British and Commonwealth L1A1, the Canadian C1 – the C1A1 variant being the most produced and widely used – was an Inch-pattern FAL offering semi-automatic only, and served as the Canadians' primary infantry rifle until 1984, when it was supplanted by the 5.56×45mm NATO C7 rifle and the C8 carbine, both based on the US AR-15. The heavy-barrelled FALO (*Fusil Automatique Lourd*, or heavy automatic rifle) version, with modified handguards, barrel, sights and magazines, became the Canadians' squad automatic weapon (SAW) in the form of the C2A1. One last Canadian FAL, often overlooked, was the C1D. This was the standard C1 rifle with the select-fire capability of the Metric FAL, offering full-automatic. It was used only by the Royal Canadian Navy, to give boarding parties automatic firepower without the extra weight and bulk of the C2A1. Canadian variants of the FAL were domestically manufactured under licence by Canadian Arsenals Ltd of Long Branch, Ontario.

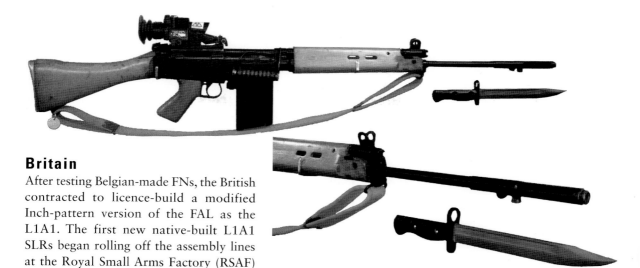

Britain

After testing Belgian-made FNs, the British contracted to licence-build a modified Inch-pattern version of the FAL as the L1A1. The first new native-built L1A1 SLRs began rolling off the assembly lines at the Royal Small Arms Factory (RSAF) Enfield in early 1957, but some Belgian-made FN rifles were used by British forces before production started. The weapon was also manufactured in a variety of other locations including Birmingham Small Arms Ltd (BSA) and Royal Ordnance Factory (ROF) Fazakerley. British-made L1A1s were exported to Brunei, Jamaica and Malaysia as well as to Rhodesia until that country made its Unilateral Declaration of Independence on 11 November 1965 and consequently became the subject of a British arms embargo.

Originally, L1A1 furniture (forearm, stock, carrying handle and pistol grip) was made of walnut wood, but this was eventually replaced with synthetic furniture. A fibreglass and nylon composite known by the brand name of Maranyl, it is identifiable by its 'pebbled' texture meant to provide a more secure grip for soldiers in the field. This was not accomplished in one fell swoop, but often over years as older stocks were replaced as needed.

British forces never adopted the heavy-barrelled SAW version of the FAL, preferring to keep the L4 7.62x51mm version of the famous Bren gun. After three decades of use across the world, the L1A1 was replaced in British service by the 5.56×45mm SA80, a select-fire bullpup assault rifle outwardly resembling the ill-fated EM-2, from 1985 onwards.

TOP: A British L1A1 SLR with wooden stock and L2A2 SUIT sight. (TM Archive)

INSET: The SLR's L1 knife bayonet, which was fitted over the flash hider with a simple bayonet lug. (TM Archive)

For the British Army's troop trials of the FAL, Fabrique Nationale produced 4,000 7.62mm X8E1 rifles, and they were issued during operations against the Mau Mau in Kenya. Here, the first and second soldiers carry X8E1s, while the others carry a 9mm Mk V Sten and two .303 Lee-Enfield No.5 'jungle carbines'. (IWM MAU 587)

15

Australia and New Zealand

The Australians and New Zealanders also called the FAL the L1A1. The Australian L1A1, with some small differences from the Canadian version, was initially manufactured in Canada, and then in Australia at the Small Arms Factory at Lithgow, New South Wales. From 1988 the L1A1 was replaced in Australian service by the 5.56×45mm F88 Austeyr, a modified version of the Austrian Steyr AUG manufactured under licence in Australia. New Zealand, having bought Australian-made L1A1s for three decades, also switched to the 5.56×45mm Austrian assault rifle in 1988, adopting the Steyr AUG model (see under 'Austrian StG 58 and variants' below). Australian-made L1A1 rifles were also exported to Papua New Guinea and Singapore.

Lithgow also manufactured the heavy-barrelled SAW model, designated the L2A1; this was identical to the Canadian C2A1, and was found by the Australians to be unsatisfactory. In the years before the Vietnam War, the Australians developed a new, upgraded weapon known as the X1F2A2 Automatic Rifle; this never reached the field as Australia decided to adopt a US weapon, the 7.62×51mm M60 GPMG (general-purpose machine gun), instead.

Germany

The post-war Bundeswehr (Federal Defence Force), was founded on 12 November 1955. It gladly adopted the FAL as the G1 ('G' standing for *Gewehr*, or rifle), purchasing some 100,000 FN-produced weapons that entered service in 1956. The G1 had user modifications similar to the Austrian StG 58 (see below) such as light metal handguards and an integral folding bipod. Like the Austrians, the Germans did not adopt the heavy-barrelled FAL, preferring to employ the MG3 (a modernized version of the famous MG42) in 7.62×51mm calibre as its GPMG.

West Germany adopted the FN FAL as the G1 rifle in 1956, but was forced to buy FN-made rifles rather than licence-producing their own. After buying 100,000 Belgian rifles, West Germany instead chose to develop and manufacture a Mauser/CETME design, which became Heckler & Koch's famous G3. Photographed in 1960, this G1 has been relegated to cadet use. (DoD)

The Germans were eminently happy with the weapon and wished to produce it themselves under licence. The Belgians would have none of it, however, having so recently suffered five years of Nazi rule, and insisted that the Germans only purchase Belgian-made FALs. Under German occupation, FN had been taken over by the major German armaments manufacturer Deutsche Waffen- und Munitionsfabriken (DWM), its directors arrested, and the assembly lines run by slave labour after only 10 per cent of the Belgian factory workers showed up when ordered to do so. After the Allies invaded Normandy in 1944, the Germans stripped the FN factories of everything useful and sent it back to augment German industries, wrecking what they couldn't take with them. FN tried to get back on its feet immediately after liberation near the end of 1944, refurbishing Allied weapons and making cheap, easily produced spare parts such as tank tracks. Adding insult to injury, the Germans later tried to destroy the factory with V1 flying bombs, achieving two direct hits. These memories were all too fresh in 1956.

For political and economic reasons, as well as national pride, the Germans insisted upon a weapon they could manufacture domestically. Thus, the Germans instead found themselves looking to a design developed by the Spanish government's Centro de Estudios Técnicos de Materiales Especiales (CETME). The CETME design was a late-war Mauser-designed assault rifle that never developed past the prototype phase before the end of World War II. Like the FAL, it was originally chambered in the wartime 7.92×33mm *kurz* calibre, and was intended to be a true assault rifle. The later 'Type A' ammunition was dimensionally identical to the 7.62×51mm NATO, but used a much-reduced powder charge and lighter bullet to make it more controllable in full-automatic fire.

Working with the Germans, the Spanish adopted the NATO 7.62×51mm cartridge, and a slightly modified version of the weapon went on to be manufactured in West Germany by Heckler & Koch (H&K) as the G3, beginning in 1959. The G3 was to become the second most popular military battle rifle – as opposed to assault rifle – in the Free World, used by some 50 nations and licence-manufactured in a dozen. Without the G3, the FAL may have completely dominated the militaries of the West during the Cold War. The majority of the German G1s were sold as surplus to the Turkish Army in the mid-1960s.

Austria

One of the favourites among today's FAL shooters is the Austrian StG 58, which is similar to the German G1. The Österreichisches Bundesheer (Austrian Armed Forces), founded in its present-day form in May 1955, initially purchased 20,000 FN-built rifles made to their own particular specifications in 1958, then contracted to licence-build their own at the Steyr plant of Steyr-Daimler-Puch.

The StG 58 features lightweight metal handguards and its own integral folding bipod which, when not in use, fits snugly and flush into slots in the bottom of the handguards. The handguards quickly became too hot to touch after prolonged firing, however. The use of plastic furniture instead of wood for the butt stock, pistol grip and carrying handle was intended to reduce weight, but the StG 58 is still a heavy weapon even for a FAL, at about 4.5kg (10lb) unloaded.

A very interesting feature is the Steyr flash suppressor. In addition to serving as a flash suppressor, its ribbed design and 22mm (0.9in) diameter also allowed the StG 58 to fire rifle grenades without any modifications or adapters, and the four-pronged open front of the suppressor could also be used as a wire cutter.

The StG 58 was replaced by the 5.56×45mm StG 77, a bullpup assault-rifle design also known as the AUG (*Armee-Universal-Gewehr*, or Universal Army Rifle), from 1977; this weapon was also built by Steyr.

An StG 58. This Austrian FAL variant has an integral folding bipod and metal handguards, and just visible is its four-pronged flash suppressor. Thanks to the 7.62mm NATO round's range and punch, the StG 58 remained in service with the elite Jagdkommando until the mid-1990s – nearly two decades after its 5.56mm replacement, the Steyr AUG, came into service. (Clyde Frogg-PD)

Argentina has exported its domestically produced FALs to other South American states. Here, a Bolivian soldier stands guard, armed with a folding-stock FAL. (SSgt Kenrick R. Thomas/DoD)

Venezuela, Argentina and Brazil

The FAL proved particularly popular in South America. One of the first and most unusual South American FAL purchases involved Venezuela, which in 1954 ordered 5,000 FN-made FALs in the little-known 7×49.15mm Optimum 2 calibre. Like the British .280in round, this cartridge was much closer to being a true intermediate round than the 7.62×51mm NATO cartridge was. Other Venezuelan modifications included a three-pronged flash hider and a locally designed rear disc sight. Later, Venezuela also adopted the 7.62×51mm NATO and the first 5,000 rifles procured were rebarrelled to that calibre.

Argentina had ordered FN-made FALs, officially adopting the weapon in 1955 and commencing negotiations with FN to manufacture their own, but the chaos following the overthrow of General Juan Perón as President of Argentina that November delayed licensing until 1958, with FN-manufactured FALs only arriving late that year. The Argentines retained the acronym FAL, as in Spanish the rifle was termed the *Fusil Automático Liviano*. The state-owned Dirección General de Fabricaciones Militares (DGFM) arms factory at Rosario eventually produced standard-model FALs plus two folding-stock 'Para' models – one with the standard-length barrel (533mm, or 21in) and the other, for special troops, with the so-called 'super-short' 436mm (17.2in) barrel – as well as the heavy-barrelled FN 50.41 SAW, known in Spanish as the FAP (*Fusil Automático Pesado*). Some 150,000 weapons were manufactured by DGFM, although an estimated 15 per cent of Argentina's military weapons were made by FN in the 1970s. Argentine-made FALs have been widely exported throughout South and Central America, to Bolivia, Colombia, Honduras, Peru and Uruguay.

Brazil was particularly pleased with the FN FALs it purchased from Belgium. The Brazilians, too, contracted to produce their own FAL, the M964, from 1964. Although the M964 was exclusively produced by Fábrica de Armas de Itajubá, one of many subsidiaries of Brazil's gigantic Indústria de Material Bélico do Brasil (IMBEL), FAL parts manufactured in Itajubá are commonly identified using the IMBEL label. IMBEL eventually produced a wide variety of different models of the FAL, including:

- the standard rifle, offering either select-fire capability (M964) or semi-automatic only (M964 MD2)

- a carbine-length barrel with the same fire options (M964 MD1 and M964 MD3, respectively)
- a folding-stock 'Para' model with standard-length barrel offering either select-fire capability (M964A1) or semi-automatic only (M964A1 MD2)
- a folding-stock 'Para' model with carbine-length-barrel, again offering either select-fire capability (M964A1 MD1) or semi-automatic only (M964A1 MD3).

Like Argentina, Brazil also adopted the heavy-barrelled version as the FAP (in Portuguese, *Fuzil Automático Pesado*).

Brazilian IMBEL receivers are well respected for their quality and have become the standard for American firms and gunsmiths to use to assemble complete FALs for today's shooting public. Perhaps a quarter of million M964s were made before work began in the early 1980s on the new MD series of weapons, essentially a FAL rebuilt to use the 5.56×45mm NATO round. The folding-stock MD-2 and the fixed-stock MD-3 were adopted in 1985, and remain in service today.

Over two decades, the Brazilian state-run arms manufacturer Fábrica de Armas de Itajubá produced around 250,000 FAL rifles under licence from FN. These Brazilian Army soldiers from the Ipiranga Special Border Platoon, carry the M964A1 folding-stock version of the FAL. (USAF MSgt Adam M. Stump/ DoD)

Indian soldiers pay tribute at the annual Martyrs' Day in New Delhi, 2011. The Ishapore Rifle Factory has manufactured the 1A version of the FAL since 1960, and along with De Santos Arms of the United States and Brazil's IMBEL, it is one of the three firms still manufacturing new FALs. (© STR/epa/Corbis)

India

Another strange FAL twist too often overlooked by Western historians involved the newly independent state of India, whose armed forces were still equipped with the .303in No. 1 Mk III* Lee-Enfield into the mid-1950s. In 1958 the American 7.62×51mm AR-10 and 5.56×45mm AR-15 rifles were tested to the satisfaction of the Indian military, but politics and old ties to Britain led to the adoption of the 7.62×51mm NATO cartridge and the FN FAL in 1963.

The Indian Armament Research & Development Establishment (ARDE) ordered several Metric-pattern FALs from FN, as well as multiple examples of both British and Australian Inch-pattern L1A1s. These rifles were minutely dissected and tested, and the Indian Army was brought on board with the new FAL.

Seeking to manufacture their own version of the FAL domestically, the Indian military was soon butting heads with FN. The Belgian firm insisted that the Indians purchase Belgian FN machinery to manufacture the rifles and hire Belgian FN technicians to run the show. These requirements seemed a little insulting to the Indians, as the Ishapore Rifle Factory had been in the business of gun-making for a century; the Indians also felt that FN was demanding far too much money in the way of licensing payments and royalties for each rifle produced. India was not a wealthy nation and had an infantry-heavy army, the sixth largest in the world at that time, which of course required a great many rifles, involving a correspondingly large expenditure of money.

So, ARDE's Small Arms Design Group began drawing up plans for their own weapon, incorporating what suited their military needs best by using their existing FALs and L1A1s as patterns. Thus, the resultant 1A was a mixture of Inch- and Metric-pattern components. As a consequence, most Indian parts are not interchangeable with either Metric-pattern FALs or Commonwealth Inch-pattern SLRs. Manufacture of the 1A began at the Ishapore Rifle Factory in 1960.

This move, of course, did not sit well with FN; in the Belgians' opinion, the 1A was merely an unlicensed copy of their FAL. An international row ensued. The Indian prime minister, Jawaharlal Nehru (1889–1964), apparently hadn't been aware of the dealings either, and successfully satisfied FN's complaints by purchasing additional standard FALs, FALOs and 60.20 GPMGs manufactured by FN in Belgium.

The Ishapore Rifle Factory initially produced the 1A at a rate of 750 rifles per week, with gradual increases, until it was replaced in Indian service from 1998 by the locally designed 5.56×45mm INSAS (Indian Small Arms System). The 1A still remains in limited production for the export market, however.

The 1A offers semi-automatic fire only, like the British L1A1. A select-fire version, the 1C, was made primarily to be a port-firing weapon in the Sarath infantry fighting vehicle (IFV), an Indian-manufactured version of the Soviet BMP-2. Despite the purchase of some heavy-barrelled FALs from Belgium, the Indian Army's SAW of choice remained the L4 version of the Bren gun in 7.62×51mm calibre, some of which are still in service with various units.

Israel

The fledgling Israel Defense Forces (IDF) adopted the FN FAL – alongside the locally originated 9×19mm Uzi submachine gun – in 1955 in order to standardize their infantry armament, until that date consisting of a wide variety of World War II-era weapons. They called it the *Rov've Mittan* ('rifle, self-loading'), or *Romat* for short; the heavy-barrelled version was designated the *Makle'a Kal*, or *Makleon*. As with some other nations' FALs, the Israeli rifles were originally select-fire weapons offering full-automatic fire, but they were later modified to fire semi-automatic only. The first weapons were Belgian FN-made specimens, but eventually Israel was to licence-produce the entire weapon and its magazines domestically. The *Romat* was replaced in service by the US 5.56×45mm M16 and the Israelis' own Galil – in both 5.56×45mm and 7.62×51mm – from 1972 onwards, although the *Romat* remained in Israeli production into the 1980s.

South Africa

The South African Defence Force (SADF) adopted the FAL in preference to rival weapons, including the German G3 and the US AR-10. They designated the standard fixed-stock rifle with full-length barrel and select-fire capability as the R1, the folding-stock 50.64 version as the R2, and a fixed-stock version with full-length barrel offering semi-automatic fire only as the R3. These weapons were progressively replaced from 1982 by the domestically produced 5.56×45mm R4 (select-fire, full-length rifle), R5 (carbine) and R6 (compact personal defence weapon), all based on the Israeli Galil. The South Africans adopted the heavy-barrelled version as the R1 HB.

The Netherlands

The Dutch adopted the FAL in 1961 as the *Het licht automatisch geweer*; this version offered semi-automatic only. The heavy-barrelled 50.42 version was designated the *Het zwaar automatisch geweer*. The Dutch eventually replaced the weapon with the Canadian C7 and C7A1 (see above).

An FN-made 'paratrooper' FAL, with short barrel, plastic folding stock and fixed rear sight. (Photo courtesy of Rock Island Auction Company)

IMPROVEMENTS AND MODIFICATIONS

Addressing the length issue: folding-stock and specialized versions

One of the FAL's few faults was its length; the L1A1 in particular, with its 102mm (4in)-long flash suppressor, was 1,143mm (45in) long overall. This length made it rather unwieldy for small-statured troops such as the Gurkhas, and was less than handy in thick jungle and urban environments. It also posed a particular problem for mechanized troops riding in armoured personnel carriers (APCs), airmobile units using helicopters, and especially for airborne troops. For example, Belgium's elite Régiment Para-Commando jumped from Fairchild C-119G 'Flying Boxcar' transport aircraft, which instead of a folding rear ramp had only a hatch door on either side to dive through. A full-length FAL was a tight squeeze when it came to exiting this door.

These length issues led to the adoption of several specialized FAL models, including both standard fixed-stock rifles with carbine-length barrels and folding-stock versions with various barrel lengths. The folding-stock carbines became known almost immediately as 'Para' or 'Congo' models; they included the 50.61 (full-length barrel, standard charging handle), 50.62 (458mm/18in barrel, folding charging handle), 50.63 (406mm/16in barrel, folding charging handle) and 50.64 (full-length barrel, folding charging handle, aluminium-alloy lower receiver). The folding cocking handle of the 50.62, 50.63 and 50.64 models was designed to keep it from protruding when the stock was folded. The 'Para' required more than just a folding stock, however. With the standard fixed-stock FAL's main buffer and spring located in the buttstock, the entire operating system had to be modified, including the receiver, to produce the folding-stock version.

Various military-issue FALs compared

	FAL Standard (50.00)	L1A1 SLR	FAL Standard Carbine	FAL Para (50.61)	FAL Para Carbine (50.3)	FALO LAR (50.41)
Weight	4.3kg (9.48lb)	4.3kg (9.48lb)	3.8kg (8.4lb)	3.9kg (8.6lb)	3.79kg (8.4lb)	5.95kg (13.1lb)
Barrel length	533mm (21in)	533mm (21in)	436mm (17.2in)	533mm (21in)	436mm (17.2in)	533mm (21in)
Length extended	1,090mm (42.9in)	1,143mm (45in)	993mm (39.1in)	1,095mm (43.1in)	998mm (39.3in)	1,125mm (44.3in)
Length folded	n/a	n/a	n/a	845mm (33.3in)	748mm (29.4in)	n/a

'Para' stocks are skeletal and universally fold forward sideways against the right side of the receiver. A rubber buttplate is fitted on some; quite a few civilian shooters have acquired a padded cheekpiece of some kind due to the felt recoil of the smaller tubular stock against the face when aiming and firing. Other users insist that the standard 'Para' stock is just fine, requiring only that one 'get used to' the difference.

Problems with desert conditions: the saga of the 'sand cuts'

Although the L1A1 was not yet in universal service with British forces during the Suez Crisis of 1956, reports came back from the field that the weapon had experienced numerous malfunctions due to the sand and dust of Egypt's desert environment. The IDF also had complaints about the FAL's performance in the desert. For British, Indian and Israeli troops alike, this proved to be a very serious issue.

Five members of the Nigerian Army establishing a perimeter near the old airfield north of Mogadishu, Somalia, 1993. During the 1980s the state-owned Defence Industries Corporation of Nigeria began licenced production of the FAL as the NR-1. The new rifle entered service in 1989. (US Army)

Extensive testing commenced in search of a solution to this problem. The tests were particularly harsh and realistic; fine particulate wind-blown sand was imported from Egypt for initial experiments at RSAF Enfield. By the end of 1955, Britain's ARDE believed it had come up with a cure, in the form of 'sand cuts'. Rifles modified in this fashion were then sent to Egypt for further field testing in actual desert conditions. In both locations, the rifles were blasted by 'artificial sandstorm' equipment and, in the latter, actually buried in the sand before firing.

The most obvious difference arising from these modifications can be seen on the exterior of the breech-block carrier – a series of machined cuts at 45-degree angles, taking the shape of 'WWW'. These 'inclined scraper recesses' were intended to remove sand from the action during both forward and backward strokes. The forward ends of the sliding surface were also relieved, and a pair of 30-degree chambers were machined on the inside edges of the carrier.

Similar relief modifications were made to the breech-block and the main slide of the receiver body. These changes, plus the use of graphite grease as a lubricant, appeared to cure what ailed the FAL in sandy and dusty

An SAS trooper gives medical treatment to the villagers of Falige, in the remote Yanqul Plain of Oman. The L1A1's early reliability problems in desert conditions had been remedied by the time of the Oman campaign. (IWM MH 30626)

conditions. The complaints garnered in the Suez Canal Zone were not evident when the L1A1 was used in similar harsh desert environments such as Muscat and Oman, the Radfan and Aden, Dhofar and Kuwait (in 1961, the first time Kuwait's neighbour Iraq tried to annex that country). Likewise, the FAL has since seen service with Bahrain, Cameroon, Chad, Cyprus, Djibouti, Liberia, Libya, Morocco, Nigeria, Qatar, Syria and Yemen.

The Israelis never adopted the British system of receiver and bolt-carrier 'sand cuts', but did modify the bolt and bolt handle of their FALs to make the bolt handle reciprocating. This allowed the bolt handle to be used as a forward assist to allow the shooter manually to push forward a cartridge that had failed to chamber fully.

Of course, standard operating procedures were also adapted to address this issue. The Australian Army's 1983 SLR manual features four paragraphs regarding care of the weapon in 'Abnormal Conditions'. The second paragraph lists desert conditions: 'When conditions are dry, sandy or dusty, clean and inspect more frequently to prevent the formation of rust and corrosion. Lubricate sparingly with graphite or light oil and then wipe dry. Wash brushes in soap and water and dry them before use' (Australian Army 1983: 2-23). They would experience further trouble with the FAL in the desert.

ACCESSORIES

Magazines

There were a variety of staggered-row detachable box magazines manufactured for the FAL in several countries, with the 20-round magazine being the standard. The two main varieties are 'Inch' and 'Metric'. The was designed specifically for the SLR as used by Britain and the former Commonwealth nations, while the latter was used by countries with Metric-pattern FALs. Inch-pattern SLRs can accept either Inch or Metric magazines, but Metric FALs will only accept Metric magazines.

The vast majority of FAL magazines were made of steel, with the original Belgian FN magazines finished with durable black enamel paint. Made on FN tooling, the Argentine and Brazilian magazines are nearly identical except for the finish on the magazine follower. Israeli-made magazines are the same, but bear two Hebrew characters stamped into the metal on one side. German G1 magazines, on the other hand, were made of aluminium with differing anodized finishes. While such coatings show wear quickly, these magazines were the lightest of the FAL varieties and, as noted, every ounce that can be shaved from the weight of an FAL is desirable.

Turning to Inch-pattern magazines, Canadian- and Australian-manufactured magazines were unmarked. British-made SLR magazines were stamped with part numbers, year of manufacture and a proof mark.

Although less common, a variety of 30-round magazines were manufactured for the heavy-barrelled SAW-configured FALs such as the C1A1 or the FAP. The British L4A2 30-round magazine is the most interesting. When Britain's Mk 3 and Mk 4 Bren guns were converted from .303in British to 7.62×51mm NATO ammunition as part of that weapon's conversion to the L4 model in 1954, the British modified the curved magazine to fit the SLR too; these magazines also work well in the Canadian FAL variants. Since the Bren fed from the top of the receiver, gravity assisted the feed. Inverted for use in the SLR, the magazine's springs sometimes proved to be underpowered; this problem was fixed in the field by removing the spring and stretching it. Other SLR and FAL 30-round magazines, usually unmarked, are Canadian or Australian-made; they are straight in profile and built with springs designed from the outset to feed upwards.

Sights

Old-fashioned iron sights, with a blade foresight and 'V'-notch rear sight, require the human eye to focus simultaneously in three planes, which it cannot do. Sight has to be transferred rapidly from one focal point to another. A vast improvement is offered by the aperture or 'peep-style' military-rifle sight. When looking through a sizeable rear aperture, the eye naturally centres itself in the opening where the most light is available, so that the shooter need only focus on two planes: the front sight and the target.

The military-issue aperture sights of the FAL and L1A1 are certainly good, but not quite in the same league as those of the M1 Garand and the M14. The standard rear sight is an aperture on a sliding scale graduated from 200m (219yd) to 600m (656yd). It is adjusted for windage via two screws, one on either side of the sight base. The rear-sight assembly itself is not protected from blows by the 'wings' or 'ears' found on most American rifles.

Another notable improved sight was the British and Commonwealth 'Hythe Sight'. The rear sight consists of two separate folding stems, each containing a different-sized aperture. For daytime use and long-range accuracy, the front 'tombstone' is flipped up, providing a 2mm (0.08in) hole. For night firing and also useful for quick snap-shooting at close range during the day, the smaller aperture is folded down to provide a much larger 7mm (0.28in) aperture.

'Para' FALs were equipped with a different sight; a two-position flip sight. The rear sight consisted of two different blades which could be used alternately, a sight with a large aperture zeroed to 150m (164yd) for rapid, close-range work and another blade with a small aperture and graduated for 250m (273yd) for more precise aiming at longer ranges.

THE FAL EXPOSED

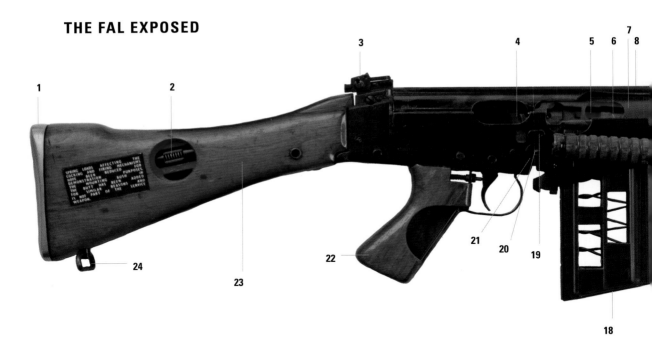

Photos © Royal Armouries, PR.10920

Operation and function

In its final form, the FAL was a gas-operated tilting-block design bearing many similarities to the World War II-era Soviet Tokarev SVT-40 self-loading rifle. Its operation can be described briefly in two sections covering the backward and forward actions of the mechanism.

The backward action

1. When the trigger is squeezed, it disengages the sear, in turn releasing the hammer to strike the end of the firing pin and fire the cartridge in the chamber.

2. As the bullet travels down the barrel, it is driven by expanding gases. A portion of these gases enters a gas vent and passes through the gas plug to force the gas piston to the rear. The piston strikes the slide and drives it rearward. Once the gas energy is expended, the gas-piston spring forces it back into the forward position.

3. As the slide is driven to the rear, it lifts the tilting breech-block up out of its locking recesses and to the rear.

4. When the breech-block moves to the rear, the empty cartridge case is pulled out of the chamber by the extractor. During rearward movement, the base of the case strikes the ejector and the empty case is ejected from the rifle.

5. In the rear position, the slide compresses its return spring, mounted within the buttstock on standard-model FALs. As the

breech-block clears the top of the magazine, the spring in the magazine pushes the next loaded round up into position for loading.

The forward action

1. The compressed return spring in the butt expands to push the breech-block and slide back into battery. As the breech-block assembly moves forward, the fresh round from the magazine is engaged and fed into the chamber.

2. As the breech-block stops its forward movement, the slide continues forward, tilting the breech-block down into the locked position for firing. The rear of the firing pin is exposed and the ejector grasps the rim of the chambered cartridge.

3. During this forward movement, the safety sear is pushed out of engagement with the hammer. The hammer then engages the trigger sear and is held there until the trigger is squeezed again.

As long as there are fresh cartridges in the magazine, this process will repeat itself every time the trigger is squeezed. On full-automatic models, the cycle will continue until the trigger is released or the magazine is empty. On 'Metric' FALs, the bolt is locked to the rear after the last round has been fired.

British Inch-pattern L23A1 instructional rifle

1. Butt plate
2. Return spring
3. Rear sight
4. Hammer
5. Ejector port
6. Breech block
7. Slide
8. Top cover
9. Handguard
10. Piston spring

11. Piston
12. Gas regulator
13. Foresight
14. Gas plug
15. Flash hider
16. Barrel
17. Carrying handle
18. Magazine
19. Locking shoulder
20. Retaining pin

21. Hinge pin
22. Pistol grip
23. Butt
24. Rear sling swivel
25. Safety sear
26. Cocking lever
27. Hammer
28. Hammer spring
29. Body locking catch
30. Body locking lever

31. Change lever
32. Trigger spring
33. Trigger plunger
34. Trigger
35. Trigger guard
36. Sear spring
37. Sear
38. Magazine catch
39. Holding open catch
40. Magazine spring

This FN-made FAL is fitted with a folding bipod, carrying handle and black composite furniture. Note the British illuminated scope, the L2A2 'Sight Unit Infantry Trilux' (SUIT) – the closest thing to an 'offical' FAL scope. (Photo courtesy of Rock Island Auction Company)

Optics

One of the main drawbacks in fitting good optics to the FAL was the design of the removable steel top cover, which was thin and had a tendency to move slightly on firing, and was unsuited to the fitting of any sight mount that required a high level of accuracy. The introduction of stronger covers and the use of side mounts that fitted to the receiver of the rifle improved matters, but it was never a particularly outstanding sniping rifle.

Nevertheless, Fabrique Nationale soon adapted the FAL to take telescopic sights, calling the weapon so outfitted *Le fusil pour tireur d'élite*, roughly translated as 'rifle for elite shooter'. Two types of scope were fitted: the OIP/FAL and the OIP/AFN, both made by Société Belge d'Optiques et d'Instruments de Précision (OIP).

The Belgian scope-mounting system used flexible metal bands tightened by bolts on a modified FAL dust cover instead of scope rings; this system held the scope low and offset to the left of the bore. The offset scope required a leather cheekpiece fitted to the stock for the shooter to achieve a good cheek weld, similar to the system used with the M1C and M1D sniper versions of the M1 Garand with their offset scope mounting. Although it was used by the Belgian Army, no other countries adopted it.

If there is an 'official' FAL scope, however, it is the Sight Unit Infantry Trilux (SUIT). In an idea rather before its time, the SUIT arose from the British and New Zealand – and later the Israeli – idea to turn the FAL platform into something akin to a designated marksman rifle (DMR). It was a good idea, and optics like the SUIT are still quite viable and effective pieces of equipment for civilian shooters, although the original SUIT has long since been surpassed in military use by newer scopes such as the Sight Unit Small Arms, Trilux (SUSAT) and Advanced Combat Optical Gunsight (ACOG).

The field manual for the SUIT summed up its form and function:

A detachable optical sight with a magnification of four, equipped with an internally illuminated inverted aiming pointer. With the sight fitted the Infantryman's night vision capability is extended enabling him to engage targets at longer distances. The amount of

The STANAG scope mount on an FN FAL. (Sedov K.B./CC-BY-3.0)

improvement depends on the light falling on the target and the target/ background contrast. The increase in range varies from two to three times that of conventional open sights. By day, the sight unit assists in the acquisition and engagement of targets with low background contrast at the effective range of the weapon to which it is attached. It also forms a useful surveillance aid. (MoD 1975: 2)

The SUIT used reflecting prisms and an offset design rather than the straight tube of conventional scopes. This configuration helped to reduce the overall size and length of the scope. Additionally, it placed the objective lens to the side of the bore, so that neither the front sight nor heat mirage from the barrel from extended firing would interfere with the view. The obvious disadvantage was parallax, in that the scope was not directly aligned over the bore, so that at some distance the bullet path and sight point of aim crossed and then departed further as range increased.

A replacement top dust cover provided the mount for the scope. The SUIT was designed to be mounted and dismounted on the weapon without the loss of zero, a claim seldom found to be 100 per cent accurate. Range estimation has long been one of the most difficult things for the infantryman to acquire accurately, but it is necessary to get the best performance from modern military rifle calibres. With the SUIT, range estimation is reduced to the question, 'Is the target closer or further away than 400m [437yd]?' Again, the manual explains succinctly: 'Adjust the range control lever as required. Use the 300m [328yd] position [to engage] targets up to 400m. Push the range control lever to the 500m position [to engage] targets between 400–600m [437–656yd]' (MoD 1975: 10).

Although the Trilux scope was used by only a few nations, the concept was not forgotten; nor did it come to be outdated. One of its greatest strengths was its 'soldier-proof' construction. It was not too surprising, therefore, that the Soviet Union 'reverse-engineered' the SUIT – with some ranging improvements – as their own 1P29 scope, which continues to be manufactured and fitted to military weapons, including the various Kalashnikovs and the PKM machine gun.

The other 'official' FAL scope was German; it was later used on the H&K G3 when West Germany's Bundeswehr adopted that weapon in place of the FAL. The Germans have long been known for high-quality glass production, and the Hensoldt Optische Werke's F-series is a fine scope with Zeiss-equivalent optics. As with most Cold War-era DMR-type scopes, it offers fixed 4× magnification, with a 24mm (0.94in) objective lens.

On the G3/HK91/CETME, the Hensoldt is mounted with the STANAG claw mount (the abbreviation stands for NATO 'Standardization Agreement'), which allows the firer to use either the scope or the regular peep sights at will. It does, however, mount the scope so high above the axis of the bore that it leaves the rifleman using a 'chin weld' rather than a 'cheek weld' with the stock, making it more difficult to achieve proper eye relief and sighting consistency.

Argentina used Hensoldt scopes on some of their FALs with a domestically designed and produced low-set scope mount that proved to be rugged and reliable. Many believe that the Argentine mount is superior

A Belgian-made FN FAL with a Hensoldt scope and (at right) a Hensoldt canvas scope case. This example is one of the 1,836 'G-Series' FN FAL rifles that were imported to the United States between 1959 and 1962. (Photo courtesy Rock Island Auction Company)

to the German STANAG mount, especially when it comes to cheek-to-stock weld.

Unlike the SUIT's simple two-position range lever, the Hensoldt has a true bullet-drop compensator (BDC) tuned exactly for the trajectory of the 7.62×51mm NATO Ball round. It is adjustable from 100m to 600m (109–656yd), and matches the trajectory very closely indeed. The Hensoldt lends itself well to more precision sniper-type shooting, as the range adjustments are in 25m rather than 100m increments. With accurate range-finding, the trajectory can be almost perfectly matched for engaging targets much smaller than man-sized – i.e. head-sized – targets. In the aftermath of the squabbles over the G1 FAL, the German Hensoldt came to be used instead on the PSG 3 ('PSG' standing for *Präzisions-Schützen-Gewehr*, or 'precision rifleman's weapon') sniper rifle, an accurized version of H&K's G3.

The Canadian Army found the C1 sufficiently accurate to develop a sniper version of the weapon. In September 1958 the Director of Infantry addressed the Royal Canadian School of Infantry with, in part, this evaluation of the Canadian-made C1's accuracy:

> In firing trials, the C1 Rifle has proved more accurate than the No. 4 Rifle at all distances up to 1,000 yards in an 'as issued' condition. The influence of wind on the bullet is less pronounced than on the .303-in Mk 7 bullet. The various features which combine to afford this greater degree of accuracy include an extremely well made barrel in addition to the cartridge characteristics. (Quoted in Stevens 1982: 125)

After a series of extensive tests conducted from October 1956 to April 1957 on American, British, Canadian and even a Russian scope, the Canadians chose the Canadian Leitz as having the superior optics and reticle.

With a new plant built in Midland, Ontario, the Leitz optics were made by the noted German Leica camera firm. Adopted as the Sniper Scope C1, it had 4× magnification and featured a BDC ring graduated from 100yd to 1,000yd in 100yd increments. Leitz also manufactured a heavy-duty top cover for the FAL to provide a solid scope-mounting base.

The British and Australian militaries both tested the Leitz and found that it fogged up in humid tropical climates. Leitz improved the sight with 'tropic proofing', and it was later accepted for service with the Australian Army. Only a few hundred of these scopes were made, and they are now valuable collector's items.

The spirit of the bayonet

The bayonet seems like an anachronism in the day of assault rifles with high-capacity magazines. The weapon itself originated centuries ago in the days of single-shot muzzle-loading muskets, when a soldier could sometimes be expected to get off only a single shot before closing with the enemy. At that point, the bayonet turned the empty musket into an efficient pike.

The British Army in particular has always placed an emphasis on cold steel. Although it seemed that the day of the bayonet had long since passed, British, Commonwealth, French and Turkish bayonets saw considerable use in the Korean War; even the tough and seemingly fearless Red Chinese infantrymen could be broken when confronted with a bayonet charge. The most famous instances of bayonet charges in modern times, however, would involve the FAL – on both sides – in vicious night fighting during the Falklands War in 1982. British forces had been fought to a standstill and the battle hung in the balance; a bayonet charge by a handful of Scots Guards against the Argentine Batallón de Infantería de Marina 5 on Mount Tumbledown tipped the scales in the British favour and carried the attack home.

The ingenious early Type A bayonet, with 'free-recoil' spring and integral flash hider. This example appears to be Argentine-made. (Joaquín Alvarez Riera-PD)

Fabrique Nationale designed the first FAL bayonet, the Type A, a standard knife-blade pattern but with an ingenious modification to keep the bayonet from affecting the rifle's accuracy while fixed. A spring hidden in the pommel of the bayonet produced what FN called a 'free-recoil' bayonet, which allowed it to 'float' while the rifle was being fired.

The early British-designed 'trident' bayonet also used FN's free-floating principle. It had been a standard practice in the British Army for decades to fix bayonets after dark. Practically from the beginning of the military issue of firearms, troops almost universally fired too high at night. The weight of a bayonet on the muzzle served as a reminder to the Tommy to fire lower at night. Since the original prototypes of the FAL did not have a muzzle device, the trident prongs of this bayonet were also intended to form a flash suppressor.

The rare, simplified Type B bayonet, which lacked the integral flash hider of the Type A. (Photo courtesy of Rock Island Auction Company)

For the SLR, the British introduced the creatively named L1A1 bayonet, and later a slightly modified L1A2, giving way to the L1A3 in the mid-1960s. Australian and Canadian blades were nearly identical to these British patterns, while the Indian 1A featured a longer blade (254mm/10in) and wooden grips. The L1 series, up to the L1A5, remained in service until 1987.

When in 1965 NATO countries standardized on muzzle devices 22mm (0.86in) in diameter in order to be able to use one another's rifle-launched grenades, a new bayonet became necessary. This became the Type C, a socket bayonet with slots to match those of the flash suppressor. It was simple, utilitarian – and ugly. It could not be used as a field knife; it was a pig sticker, plain and simple.

The Austrians, though, never developed or adopted a bayonet for their StG 58. When asked about this by an American gun writer, one Austrian colonel replied, 'Have a friend poke you in the chest just as hard as he can with the grenade launcher and see if you like it'. (Quoted in Fortier 2001: 26).

Rifle grenades

Western European and other Free World armies have always seemed to make greater use of rifle grenades than have US forces. Until the arrival of dedicated grenade launchers such as the 40mm M79 and M203, rifle-launched grenades were a common item in military inventories around the world. (The Rhodesians were limited in their choices by UN embargo, however, and apparently did not use anti-personnel rifle grenades.)

As with many other infantry weapons, the main weakness of the rifle grenade lay in the lack of live-fire training needed to become proficient with them. Soldiers in World War II, who had long experience and much practice with these grenades (usually under enemy fire, guaranteed to inspire rapid learning), spoke well of the weapon and were able to perform a wide variety of valuable tasks with them, although anti-tank use was never high on that list.

Accordingly, FN developed and manufactured a variety of rifle grenades. (The synthetic butt for the FAL itself was adopted in part because it was stronger than the wooden type and could withstand the firing of considerable numbers of grenades while supported on a hard surface.) The most widely used of the FAL rifle-launched grenades was known to most soldiers by the name 'Energa'. The Energa is an anti-tank, hollow-charge, high-explosive weapon fired from a projector fitted to a rifle, or a flash suppressor designed to fit rifle grenades. It was designed from the outset as an anti-tank weapon; its anti-personnel effect was comparatively small compared to that achieved by conventional fragmentation-type grenades.

Older rifle grenades such as the Energa required a special blank grenade-launching or ballistic cartridge; some individual weapons, such as the FAL, also required a dedicated grenade-launching projector to be attached to the muzzle of the rifle to use them. Especially with a self-loading rifle, this system was inefficient and sometimes downright dangerous to a soldier in the heat of battle trying to keep blanks and live rounds separate from one another.

The best and most efficient rifle grenade that followed the Energa was the bullet-trap (BT) grenade of the early 1960s. MECAR, another Belgian firm based in Brussels, led the development of and still manufactures the most notable BT rifle grenades, which have seen use by some 35 nations. BT rifle grenades have a steel tube in the stem; this contains a series of

hardened-steel discs. These discs absorb shock and collapse upon themselves, trapping the bullet while harnessing its power and that of the propellant gases to launch the grenade. This greatly facilitates the ease with which rifle grenades can be utilized by the ordinary rifleman, and considerably reduces recoil.

There are further types of rifle-launched grenades, equally useful but not specifically designed for anti-tank or anti-personnel use. Battlefield illumination, even for troops with some night-vision equipment, can be a godsend; at the other end of the spectrum, obscuring visibility can be equally important. A series of rifle-launched smoke grenades can create an effective screen that can conceal either an attack or withdrawal. For example, the MECAR BT smoke grenade has a range of 300m (328yd) and burns for 2½ minutes, emitting a cloud of dense opaque smoke the entire time. Rifle-launched 'riot control' grenades filled with CS tear gas also saw frequent use in Northern Ireland and Palestine for dispersing crowds of rioters or protesters.

Brazilian Army special forces during the 2003 Independence Day Parade in Brasília, Brazil. Note the tubular socket bayonets, known as the Type C, which somewhat resembled apple-corers. (Victor Soares/ABr/ CC-BY-3.0-BR)

USE
The right arm of the Free World

Oddly enough, even though it was the most widely distributed military rifle in the Free World, the FAL rifle never did see service in its intended role. Meant to face a Soviet invasion of Western Europe, the FAL fortunately never had to be used for this purpose. It did, however, give excellent service in battle around the world in many smaller wars and numerous insurgencies.

IN BRITISH SERVICE: SUEZ TO THE GULF WAR

The Malayan Emergency

Within the post-war 'End of Empire' conditions experienced by Britain, the FAL in its L1A1 form saw nearly continuous use from the 1950s to the early 1990s in a long series of counter-insurgency conflicts. The L1A1 served British and Commonwealth armies in the Malayan Emergency (1948–60), the Suez Crisis of 1956, the Indonesian Confrontation (1962–66), Vietnam, the 'Troubles' in Northern Ireland, the Falklands War of 1982 and – owing to Special Air Service (SAS) mistrust of the SA80 assault rifle – some limited use in the First Gulf War in 1991.

During the Malayan Emergency of the 1940s and 1950s, British forces were stretched thinly indeed, as units were sent to fight other communist forces in Korea. In the early days of the Emergency, bolt-action Lee-Enfield No. 5 'jungle carbines' and underpowered American-made M1 and M2 Carbines first saw initial action until replaced by the FAL. The earliest FALs to arrive in-country were of Belgian FN manufacture. Later, when UK production of the SLR geared up, the troops received genuine L1A1s. An American observer detailed his thoughts on the weapon:

Because of the British emphasis on the individual soldier and his personal weapon, small arms were of great importance. The British Army had a fine new family of predominantly 7.62 millimeter infantry weapons, as efficient and effective as any in the world for conventional warfare. For various reasons, these arms were not particularly well adapted to the jungle ...

The standard infantry rifle in the British Army and the armies of the wealthier members of the Commonwealth was the self-loading rifle designed by the Fabrique Nationale d'Armes de Guerre (FN). This is a fine weapon which fires the 7.62 millimeter NATO round, 20 to each detachable box magazine. In the British Army, this weapon does not fire fully automatically, but can deliver rapid single shots with astonishing accuracy.

It was entirely satisfactory during the Malayan emergency, but eventually ran into severe competition from the AR15 (US M16) ... For use in the jungle, the British Army felt that the AR15 was superior to their self-loading rifle ... (Weller 1966: 17)

The L1A1 SLR continued in use through Britain's 'small wars' of the late 20th century. Here, a soldier of H Squadron, 5 Royal Tank Regiment, crosses a makeshift bridge in Sarawak, North Borneo, during the Indonesian Confrontation, 1966. The original walnut furniture of the L1A1 was eventually replaced by a lighter, waterproof composite stock. (IWM FEW-66-27-35)

Militarily, the Emergency was a small-unit war, involving short, sharp firefights between small groups. The troops had to be alert and ready to fight at any moment during their 'jungle bashing', often after weeks without a single contact. From National Servicemen to Gurkhas, the soldiers responded magnificently, proving the Western soldier could indeed outperform the Third World guerrilla.

For British and Commonwealth troops involved in the Emergency, great stress was placed on marksmanship. The Anti-Terrorist Operations in Malaya (ATOM) manual *The Conduct of Anti-Terrorist Operations* in Malaya covered in detail the tactics of jungle warfare, yet always came back to good shooting as a prerequisite: 'The best plan, the best leadership, and the most skilful fieldcraft will avail nothing if the men cannot shoot to kill when they meet the CT' (British Army 1958: 15/2). Civil actions, amnesties, the 'winning of hearts and minds' and the August 1957 establishment of Malaya as an independent nation combined to make the British response to the Emergency successful. The military side of operations in Malaya was a war of a thousand cuts, and the Commonwealth forces inflicted the vast majority of them.

The British in the Middle East

In the Middle East, the L1A1 proved an ideal weapon. In places like Oman, Aden and Dhofar, where the terrain was wide open and cover scarce, long range and accuracy were needed in a service rifle. Local tribesmen were, initially at least, armed with elderly British rifles such as the accurate, hard-hitting .303in Lee-Enfield, and in some cases even the old single-shot black-powder .577/450 Martini-Henry was still in use. The tribesmen who wielded them, however, had practically grown up with these rifles in their hands and were often crack marksmen.

Operating against Saudi-backed rebels in the barren mountain massif of the Jebel Akhdar in Muscat and Oman in 1957–59, SAS troopers found using grenade launchers and the Energa on their L1A1s quite effective. When fired into a cave or thick mud-walled building occupied by insurgents, the sheer concussion of the blast contained within an enclosed area proved devastating. (Dewar 1987: 83–93)

One startling example of the value of the semi-automatic L1A1's ammunition conservation comes from the Aden Emergency (1963–67), where British forces fought a tough battle in what would become South Yemen even as the politicians were backing out of the protectorate. Soviet-made arms were being smuggled to the rebels via the rugged, rocky and nearly waterless Radfan Mountains, across terrain not unlike parts of Afghanistan.

The Edwards Patrol in April 1964 involved nine men from No. 3 Troop SAS infiltrating into enemy-occupied mountains to mark out a drop zone for a landing by the Paras in the middle of the rebels' supposedly secure backyard. Achieving the right balance between mobility and firepower is always a nagging problem for infantry. In the dry desert wastes of the rugged, burning Radfan, water was a vital necessity even more important than bullets. With water weighing 3.6kg (8lb) to the gallon, each man had to carry approximately 7.3kg (16lb) of the precious commodity.

Since Intelligence reports insisted that the patrol would be unlikely to encounter much enemy resistance and should be able to steal past the rebels without engaging in any real fighting, weight was saved in the ammunition department. Each man carried four spare magazines of 7.62×51mm NATO for his L1A1 (80 rounds), plus a 50-round bandolier of the same in his pack, as well as some extra .303in ammunition for the patrol's single Bren LMG. It was stressed that ammunition must be conserved jealously and spent wisely and effectively.

High in the mountains of South Arabia, an SLR-armed sentry from the Coldstream Guards maintains a watch on the wadi below. The range and power of the L1A1 proved its worth in the Aden campaigns. (IWM R 35178)

Captain Robin Edwards' patrol encountered problems from the beginning. As they moved through the mountains, it soon became clear that the radioman was suffering from food poisoning and unable to keep pace. Thus, dawn found the SAS men far from their destination and they were forced to take cover for the day in a couple of old enemy sangars, fighting positions made from piled stones on rocky ground that did not allow digging. As fate would have it, the men's hiding place was discovered by a goatherd in an incident eerily similar to the problem encountered by SAS team Bravo Two Zero during the First Gulf War. Local tribesmen were alerted and rushed to the scene from all directions, resulting in a day-long sniping duel between the jihadists and the SAS men. The troopers husbanded every round, shooting carefully.

A Sterling-armed Royal Anglian dog handler and his Alsatian with a patrol of L1A1-armed soldiers in the mountains of South Arabia. The Sterling provided a full-automatic, short-range complement to the semi-automatic, long-range fire of the SLR. (IWM TR 24800)

Air support, in the form of Hawker Hunter ground-attack aircraft of the Royal Air Force (RAF), came to the patrol's aid during the day and suppressed the tribesmen. As darkness fell, however, the air support was unable to continue. By then, the patrol's radioman had been killed; all of the men were wounded to one degree or another, some severely, since in the rocks of the sangar even near-misses from rifle bullets sprayed them with rock and lead fragments.

Knowing the rebels would try to overrun the patrol under the cloak of night, Captain Edwards led the break-out and escape of the SAS patrol in the darkness. He was killed in the attempt as the tribesmen, seeing their quarry escaping, swarmed after the patrol. The seven wounded survivors managed to make their way back towards British-controlled lines through the forbidding terrain. An Arab tracker and three other tribesmen were detected following the patrol's trail, and two SAS men hung back and hit the Arabs with a hasty ambush, cutting down all four with their L1A1s. Later in the night, another pair of guerrillas found and followed the patrol; they were killed in a repeat of the first ambush.

Eventually, just after daybreak, the battered and bloody survivors encountered a British armoured car, which took the two most severely wounded back to base while the last five marched home. Despite the long ordeal, day-long firefight, and two ambushes, none of the men had run completely out of ammunition. Casualties among the enemy were unknown, but must have been quite extensive. That such a small group survived at all amidst many hundreds of angry guerrillas was amazing.

Although the majority of the patrol survived this epic encounter, any good to come of it was marred when the rebels desecrated the bodies of the captain and the signaller and paraded through the streets displaying their severed heads; shades of US Army helicopter pilots in Mogadishu three decades later.

One cannot help but compare the Edwards Patrol to a more recent incident, in September 2006. Task Force 31, consisting of a company of American Special Forces and the Afghan commandos they were training, all armed with full-automatic weapons, were engaged in a firefight with insurgents. After only 20 minutes they had expended nearly all of their ammunition and were forced to break contact to resupply by helicopter. (Helicopters cannot always be available at one's beck and call for ammunition resupply, however; something the British found out in the Falklands.)

On 17 June 1967, only nine days before the British withdrew from Aden, No. 9 Troop of 45 Commando of the Royal Marines, again armed with L1A1s and a single Bren gun, had a skirmish with a handful of guerrillas. As David Young, historian of 45 Commando, recalled:

> We leapt out of the choppers, having placed our piquets – in case they tried to run away – and as we got out we saw the three men dashing up a low hill about 200 yards away. One stopped and fired at us. We were right out in the open and as there was such a din going on, I blew my whistle and told the lads to adopt a kneeling position for firing. This they did and two dissidents were killed outright, a great achievement as it is a most difficult position to fire from. The third ran over the crest of a hill and slap into the piquet commanded by Cpl. McLaughlin and was shot at 30 yds range. Throughout the entire engagement, only 80 rounds were expended … (Quoted in Geraghty 1982: 93)

Although completely unheralded by the press at the time, the battle of Mirbat on 18 July 1972 in South Oman was an epic last stand in the mould of Rorke's Drift or the Alamo. The ancient mud-walled forts of the town were garrisoned by nine SAS troopers acting as a training cadre for local troops, who were armed with a mish-mash of FN FALs, L1A1s and .303in Lee-Enfield bolt-action rifles. Other than these small arms, the only heavy weapons were a single Browning .50-calibre machine gun, a single 81mm mortar, and a World War II-vintage 25-pdr gun.

Surrounding the isolated post in the darkness came over 250 Marxist guerrillas, the best of the Dhofar Liberation Front (DLF), well armed with the latest Soviet and Chinese weapons, from AK-47s to 82mm mortars and rocket-propelled grenades. Outgunned and outnumbered more than five to one, the Omani and British forces responded magnificently to the guerrillas' attack. With so few heavy weapons, the defenders found that their SLRs and FALs played an important part in fending off the assault. Atop their 'team house', the SAS troopers fought back:

> Another of his [Captain 'Mike' Kealy's] soldiers, Trooper W., opened up with the Browning, raking the area between the two forts, while others, firing from the roof of the BATThouse [headquarters of the

British Army Training Team], picked off targets with careful precision with FN automatic rifles and a light machine gun.

Throughout the confusion, Corporal B. calmly indicated targets for the SAS mortar, the Browning, and light machine-guns, using lines of tracer to emphasize his fire orders. He also picked off leading guerrillas with his own rifle. (Geraghty 1982: 145)

The most amazing story of the battle involved Sergeant Talaisi Labalaba, a broad-shouldered Fijian trooper with massive strength. He manned the isolated 25-pdr gun, doing the job of an artillery crew alone. As the Adoo guerrillas closed, Sergeant Labalaba was actually aiming down the bore of the artillery piece before slamming home a shell and firing. All of his mates attributed their success in holding the post to his single-handed stand with the 25-pdr. He was finally killed in action at the 25-pdr, and yet was awarded only a posthumous Mention in Dispatches when many felt he had earned the Victoria Cross. At the time, however, the British government did not wish the public to know of British soldiers involved in direct combat in Oman and the incident was hushed up.

Armed with L1A1s, two lance-corporals of the Parachute Regiment in Aden outside the charred remains of a Jewish synagogue, which was set on fire during rioting in 1965. (IWM ADN 65-513-6)

Eventually, the thick, low cloud ceiling cleared just enough for Omani jet aircraft to strafe the rebels and for helicopters to land SAS reinforcements. The guerrillas broke off their attack, leaving casualties and large amounts of new Soviet-made equipment across the battlefield. The battle effectively broke the back of the DLF.

Nearly 25 years later at the dawn of a new century, the Omani Army was newly re-equipped with Steyr AUG bullpup assault rifles in 5.56×45mm. It did not take a new generation of guerrillas long to determine the limitations of the 5.56mm round. Omani Jeep and Land Rover patrols soon found themselves being engaged from long range by tribesmen with Lee-Enfields. Disabling the vehicles with the powerful .303in British rounds, the guerrillas could then pick off the soldiers at their leisure from beyond the effective range of the troops' AUGs. The AUGs were eventually transferred to rear-echelon security troops and the field troops were re-equipped with the 'old' H&K G3 battle rifle in 7.62×51mm.

Troops of 1 Para on patrol in Cupar Street, Belfast in August 1969, armed with walnut-stocked L1A1 SLRs.
(IWM TR 32986)

The Troubles

The so-called 'Troubles' in Northern Ireland were a thankless no-win situation for all involved, not least the British soldiers sent there in 1969 to keep the peace. Well before the US Marine Corps came up with the phrase 'Strategic Corporal', at least one British officer called internal-security operations in Northern Ireland the 'Corporal's War'[1]. As with other lessons learned and relearned in urban warfare, the situation in Belfast and elsewhere called for precise individual marksmanship rather than massed overwhelming firepower and supporting arms, a fact which sadly was learned once more in places like Baghdad, Fallujah and even Kabul. The 4× SUIT scope was developed in part to help soldiers in Northern Ireland with target identification as well as accuracy, as the following commentary noted:

> Shooting incidents are likely to occur when they are least expected. Reaction, which must be immediate and automatic, requires the fourth attribute of good internal security operations, the skilful and proper use of personal weapons. Accuracy of returned fire is essential; only too often, the target is a fleeting one and may be masked by women and children. Single shot is normally used, and all must be carefully aimed. Telescopic and night sights are issued, but the principal reliance is placed upon individual competence. Even infantry units have to re-learn their traditional skills as marksmen on the classification ranges before being assigned to Northern Ireland. (Dodd 1976: 58)

This tradition of good shooting would stand the British Army in good stead in other places, especially the Falkland Islands, and the SLR was able to deliver what was required.

1   That is, due to the increasingly complex, urbanized and politicized nature of war, junior non-commissioned officers may find themselves making small-unit military decisions which can have global repercussions.

THE FAL IN AFRICA

The Congo crisis

For many, the FN FAL made its debut on the world stage by appearing in photographs and film footage of the fighting in the former Belgian Congo. Many former European colonies in Africa, upon gaining their independence, degenerated into chaos and tribal warfare. Into this mix was added communism, which became a powerful force as various communist countries sent huge amounts of armaments – and advisors – to the largest groups of guerrillas.

In 1964, communist-backed guerrillas calling themselves Simbas took over large parts of the Congo from the fledgling nationalist government under Moïse Tshombe (1919–69). The Simbas killed off the intelligentsia and committed many other atrocities as well, especially involving European mission workers, including nuns. In the town of Stanleyville (now Kisangani), the Simbas took a large number of civilians hostage; these were mainly white Europeans but also included some Congolese friendly to the government.

A Congolese soldier resting in the bush, 1961. He is armed with a Belgian FN FAL. (Photo by Terrence Spencer/Time Life Pictures/Getty Images)

Due to the ongoing bloodshed and the fear that the hostages would be executed, a rescue mission was planned, Operation *Dragon Rouge*, involving the crack Belgian troops of the 1er Régiment de Para-Commando. The Belgian Air Force was, at the time, equipped with American-made Fairchild C-119G 'Flying Boxcars' and it was found that the extensive length of the standard FAL rifle could prove difficult for paratroops exiting the aircraft. In early 1964, the Régiment Para-Commando had begun to receive a new weapon, a modified FAL with a folding stock to make it more compact. Not all para-commandos were equipped with the new weapon, but its initial use in Operation *Dragon Rouge* would lead to it forever being referred to as the 'Para' or 'Congo' FAL.

At 0400hrs on 24 November 1964, some 350 para-commandos made a 'hot' (opposed) parachute drop onto Stanleyville airport. Within 40 minutes they had secured the airfield and removed obstacles from the runway. This enabled the five US Lockheed C-130 Hercules aircraft carrying more Belgian troops to land at the airfield. No fewer than five rebel counter-attacks were beaten off by the para-commandos at the airfield, while another advance group fought its way into Stanleyville proper.

On the ground, Congolese troops and a band of mostly white mercenaries known as 5 Commando was likewise rushing towards Stanleyville. These were the troops of colourful Irish soldier-of-fortune Colonel 'Mad Mike' Hoare, hired by Tshombe. The first action of the mercenaries had proven near disastrous, as some of Hoare's men were not the fully trained veteran soldiers they claimed to be.

Hoare's 5 Commando then conducted serious military training to weed out the undesirables and bring the unit together. Much of that training involved live-fire practice at a home-made rifle range with the new weapon issued to the mercenaries – the FN FAL rifle. Hoare himself was particularly impressed by the weapon and greatly appreciated the full-automatic capability for jungle warfare: 'Every man who was armed with an FN rifle … was now the equivalent of a light machine-gunner, restricted only by the amount of ammunition he could carry or had immediate access to. With this firepower, four men with FN rifles were a potent force' (Hoare 2008: 16).

As with just about everyone else who used the FAL, Hoare's men found the weight of the weapon was an issue. It was impossible not to become weary carrying a 4.5kg (10lb) rifle all day and the regulation military sling could not keep the weapon in the 'ready' position. The mercenaries quickly figured out that the longer sling taken from the AK-47 could be jury-rigged into a useful assault sling – and the Simbas provided them with as many AK-47s as they could pick up off the ground.

Assaulted from the air and pushed from the ground, the Simbas in Stanleyville brought their civilian hostages out into the street and killed many of them literally within minutes of the arrival of the para-commandos. The liberated survivors were treated and flown out to the safety of the capital, Léopoldville (now Kinshasa).

Rhodesia

During the so-called Bush Wars in Rhodesia (1964–1979) the FN FAL was the favoured and most numerous weapon in the hands of the Rhodesian Security Forces. As with the counter-insurgency in Malaya, the Rhodesians took a 'quality over quantity' approach. In this case, they really had no other choice; the United Nations had embargoed the country. Thus, their heavy firepower was limited to some old 25-pdr artillery pieces, a few armoured cars and some generally obsolescent aircraft. Most of the Security Forces consisted of light infantry, and they were without a doubt the best light infantry in modern history; even the regular infantry formations could be considered elite. These included the Rhodesian Light Infantry, the King's African Rifles, Gray's Scouts and the Selous Scouts. With the vast majority of actions being small-unit infantry engagements, the trooper's rifle and his ability to use it became particularly important. The standard small unit of the Security Forces was the stick, which consisted of four men: three riflemen armed with some version of the FAL, and one machine gunner carrying an FN MAG-58 machine gun.

Due to the international sanctions against the country, the Rhodesian government gladly accepted any weapons they could get. They were originally equipped with British-made L1A1s. Later, their FAL arsenal would include the German G1 version and the South-African-built R1.

As had the Malayan ATOM manual (many of those serving in Rhodesia were indeed veterans of the Malayan Emergency), the Rhodesian Anti-Terrorist Operations (ATOPS) manual stressed the need for the individual soldier to deliver quick and accurate rifle fire. One of the 'main requirements for success' was:

Rhodesian troops on operations in the Bush Wars, 1968. The Rhodesian security forces were originally supplied with L1A1 rifles, but after the Unilateral Declaration of Independence in 1965 only South Africa supplied arms – including the South African-made R1 select-fire FAL. (Photo by Monks/*Express*/Getty Images)

Snap shooting. The vital importance of accurate and quick shooting from all positions and all types of cover.
The two most important training requirements are supreme physical fitness and the ability to shoot accurately at fleeting targets at short and medium ranges. (Rhodesian Security Forces 1975: 35)

While many of the Rhodesian FALs, excluding the L1A1s, were capable of full-automatic fire, semi-automatic was still generally favoured. Veteran and gun writer the late Dave Arnold explained why:

Like most of the Rhodesian Security Forces, the change lever on my FN was set for semi-auto only. I had the option of having this changed to include full auto, but I decided against it. Through practice, I could put down a devastating barrage of accurate semi-automatic fire that just could not be matched on full auto. I have never had much faith in full automatic fire capability in a full bore battle rifle, simply because you generally waste ammunition without hitting anything after the first shot has been fired. The recoil generated by the powerful 7.62mm NATO round makes the gun virtually impossible to control unless shots can be restricted to short two and three-round bursts. (Arnold 1987: 66)

A considerable number of H&K G3 battle rifles also found their way to the country, but these were used mostly by reserve and other non-frontline forces, while the men at the sharp end almost universally preferred the FAL. Although their ability to continually defeat opponents who greatly outnumbered them flew in the face of conventional military wisdom, it was not enough, and international political realities eventually caused the downfall of Rhodesia's white minority regime.

South Africa

Of necessity, like those of Rhodesia, the SADF had to take a quality-over-quantity approach with their armed forces, creating some of the best light infantry in the world via tough, intensive training and two years of universal, mandatory military service. Many veterans of the Rhodesian Wars joined their ranks after Rhodesia became Zimbabwe in 1980.

Technically, South Africa was at peace during the 1970s and 1980s, but in effect the government was waging a seemingly endless counter-insurgency. Nigeria, Angola and other countries sent guerrillas to attack inside the South African border, trained by Cuban troops and armed with the latest Soviet Bloc military arms. As in Rhodesia, the FAL in well-trained hands proved superior to the AK-47 in poorly trained hands, and most actions were marked by relatively small groups of South African soldiers inflicting a disproportionately high number of casualties on numerically superior enemies.

Rhodesian police reservists undergo weapons training with FN FALs, in the months before the 1979 election that ended the Bush Wars. Men aged between 50 and 60 were called up to ensure order in towns during the election. (AFP/Getty Images)

Angola

The Portuguese also used the FAL in their former colonies in Africa. Even though their standard infantry weapon upon modernization became the H&K G3 rifle, there were also some Belgian-made FALs and German G1 FALs in the inventory. The FAL became the favoured weapon for elite counter-insurgency special-forces units such as the Caçadores Especiais ('Special Hunters').

THE ARAB–ISRAELI WARS

The FAL had first gone to war during the Suez Crisis of 1956 – a handful in British service as well as a small number serving with the IDF. The Israeli FAL, known as the *Romat*, would serve through both the 1967 Six-Day War and the 1973 Yom Kippur War as the IDF's issue infantry rifle.

The FAL failed to make an impact in terms of public perception during the Arab–Israeli Wars; daring precision jet aircraft strikes and high-speed tank warfare across the open desert made the headlines. For the infantry in general and the paratroopers in particular, it was the famous Uzi submachine gun that possessed the 'sex appeal' to be most often seen in movies and photographs. The Uzi was at the time perhaps the best submachine gun in the world. Compact and reliable, with its 32-round magazine and cyclic rate of fire of 600rds/min, its firepower proved invaluable in the paratroops' night assaults and in urban infantry battles.

In the desert, however, the Uzi's 9×19mm Parabellum ammunition launched from a 260mm (10.23in) barrel quickly ran out of range and power. Ariel Sharon himself made note of this after the famous battle for the Mitla Pass during the 1956 Sinai campaign. Trying to fight their way out of an Egyptian ambush in the pass, his paratroops '... mounted the ridge and began to fight on it. When they reached the top of the ridge, the enemy opened strong fire with medium and light weapons from the ... ridge opposite, and from the caves. The [Israeli] unit was equipped in general with submachine guns [and] did not have weapons capable of returning the enemy fire'. (Luttwak & Horowitz 1975: 158).

For the Israeli Army, which had formerly been getting by with a variety of rifles from different sources and in different calibres, the *Romat* and the heavy-barrelled *Makleon* SAW would provide standardization on an unprecedented scale in the IDF, not only sharing a universal calibre, but magazines and parts as well. It would seem to have been a soldier's and, even more so, a quartermaster's dream come true.

The American military historian Brigadier General S.L.A. Marshall interviewed many Israelis shortly after the 1956 Suez/Sinai conflict and the Six-Day War of 1967, observing how the Israeli infantry operated, and how they incorporated all the weapons in their arsenal into their tactics. He refers to the heavy-barrelled *Makleon* SAW as an LMG:

Israel Army [*sic*] is built up around an eight-man infantry section, the leader of which carries a submachine gun as does one other man. There are also two light machine guns with the section and four riflemen, one of whom is a specialist antitank grenadier.

In its attack formation during daylight, the section moves with the leader, the grenadier and one machine gunner forward as a three-man point. The others are deployed some paces to the rearward, two men on one flank, three on the other ...

The Israeli heavy-barrelled *Makleon* FAL with hinged buttplate.

By Israeli training practice, when the light machine guns are used as a fire base to cover the forward movement of the rest of the section, they should not operate at more than two hundred yards' maximum range from the target. To cut that distance by half is considered better. In the attack LMGs are rated as highly expendable items and are shoved far front. When the section rushes the enemy position under cover of the LMG fire, one rifleman stays back to protect the gunners.

Rifle and LMG ammunition are interchangeable. There are sixty magazines carried within the squad, twenty bullets to a clip, or twelve hundred rounds altogether. (Marshall 1958: 241)

The paratroopers were considered the elite of Israeli ground troops, and operated most often as light infantry. Operating out of range of supporting fire, often without air cover, and specializing in night assaults, the paratroopers fielded an eclectic mix of firepower to handle any situation:

More than 50 percent of Israel's paratroops now have the Uzi submachine gun which is probably the best weapon of its type anywhere ... At squad level, there are, at least three 7.62mm NATO rifles, usually two semiautomatic FN rifles and one similar weapon with a heavy barrel, a bipod and a fully automatic capability. One of the men equipped with a FN rifle generally has sniper training and sometimes a telescopic sight. All paratroops in Israel take pride in being able to shoot accurately themselves and most units have at least one real marksman. (Weller 1973: 49)

The telescopic sight mentioned was, of course, the Israeli-manufactured version of the 4× SUIT. Users served more in the capacity of designated marksmen – less highly trained than real snipers, and operating within a squad rather than independently.

The IDF has long been fond of the rifle grenade. For night assaults on prepared defensive positions, Israeli infantry often crept to within rifle-grenade range. The assault was started with a volley of grenades onto the enemy positions intended to stun them and put their heads down, immediately followed by the infantry assault before their opponents could recover. In such assaults, close-range volume firepower from weapons such as the Uzi was preferable to that offered by the *Romat*. As far back

IDF troops attack the Jordanian-controlled West Bank village of Samua, 1960s. Three soldiers are armed with Uzis (the soldier in the centre is reloading), while their prone comrade has a heavy-barrelled *Makleon* for light support. (Cody Images)

as the 1960s, S.L.A. Marshall noted: 'Israel's infantry prefers the rifle-fired antitank grenade to the bazooka for shock effect on a group or bunker. At night, if the section should run into an ambush, the grenadier fires and all the others rush straight in, not firing'. (Marshall 1958: 241)

At first, Israel manufactured a copy of the Energa rifle grenade for use with their FALs. Other, more recent designs are still in production. A good example is the Israeli-made BT/AT 52. This is a BT rifle grenade that can be used from 5.56mm or 7.62mm weapons, which share the same-diameter muzzle device, with a maximum range of 300m (328yd) from the latter.

The Israeli doctrine of using tanks to kill tanks left the infantry ill-equipped with anti-tank weapons. One Israeli strongpoint guarding the Golan Heights during the Syrian armoured attacks there in 1973 had only a single bazooka and five rockets for it. When these were expended, a young Israeli lieutenant engaged five Soviet-made Syrian T-62 tanks with his *Romat* and rifle grenades, although doubtful of their capabilities. He hit the first two tanks and although there were no Hollywood-style fuel-air explosions, both tanks stopped moving and stopped firing. The other three forced the lieutenant back to the cover of the underground fortifications. (Rabinovich 2004: 212)

Although much has been made about Egyptian use of AT-3 'Sagger' wire-guided anti-tank missiles, in 1973 Israeli armour also suffered heavily from the now ever-present RPG-7 shoulder-launched anti-tank missile. Well-camouflaged Egyptian commandos, operating behind the lines, laid ambushes along the routes taken by Israeli reinforcements and fired large numbers of RPGs. When scattered by the surviving tanks, they often regrouped in the dark and would lay another ambush. Israeli tankers were also surprised by the regular Egyptian infantryman of 1973; he was not the infantryman of 1967. The latter had often fled when Israeli tanks penetrated their lines, but his successor held his ground against armour and fired large numbers of RPGs. Only friendly infantry could put them out of action for good.

An Israeli soldier during the Six-Day War, 1967. Although much less celebrated as an Israeli service weapon than the Uzi submachine gun, the FN FAL played a significant role in the Israeli infantry for two decades. (© Henri Bureau/Sygma/Corbis)

49

It was the IDF in the Sinai, much more so than UK troops in the Suez, who first encountered problems with the FAL in a desert environment. Later, the story of the FAL experiencing extreme problems in the desert grew to become 'common knowledge' among the military and shooting community. Just how bad was the problem? It is hard to find actual after-action reports quantifying the malfunctions and jams in a desert environment. At one end of the spectrum Yisrael Galil (1923–95), who happened to build the *Romat's* replacement, claimed to have seen piles of killed Israeli soldiers with jammed and useless FALs clenched in their hands. At the other end, American gun writers of the 1980s told horror stories (always second-hand, of course) of poorly trained Israeli reservists and conscripts tossing their FALs to the ground from the top of their vehicles and never bothering to clean them.

The truth, no doubt, lies somewhere between the two extremes. Riding in open-topped half-tracks in armoured columns stretching for miles, the tank tracks filling the air with an endless cloud of dust full of fine grit, and leaping from their half-tracks to hit the sand, the Israeli armoured infantry would have found their weapons filthy at the moment of contact. In the lightning-fast mobile combat the Israelis engaged in, soldiers hardly had time to eat and went days without sleep; there is not always time for constant weapons cleaning. As one joker put it, when exposed to enough desert dust and sand, any man-made machine short of a claw-hammer will stop functioning eventually.

The FAL began to be replaced by the Israeli-designed and -manufactured Galil assault rifle in 1974. Based upon the Kalashnikov rotating-bolt mechanism and the Garand trigger mechanism, the Galil used the Finnish M62 assault rifle as a basis for the receiver; this combination offered durability and reliability under the roughest of conditions. During both training and war, some Israeli soldiers had been observed using the feed lips of rifle magazines as bottle openers, itself a habit not conducive to good weapon functioning. When Israeli Military Industries (IMI) introduced the new Galil rifle, it featured a bottle opener on the bipod to prevent this problem, and that feature seemed to fascinate the press and the shooting world.

Whatever the case of the desert FAL – junk or gem, misused or incapable – it did equip the IDF for two decades and contributed to Israeli victory in two major modern wars.

The FAL in action alongside its Israeli replacement, the Galil assault rifle – but a long way from the Middle East. This photo of two Sandinista guerillas was taken on 6 June 1979 as they fought to overthrow the Somoza government. Their rifles are recently captured from the Nicaraguan National Guard. (Archives UPI/AFP/Getty Images)

THE INDO-PAKISTANI WARS

In the aftermath of World War II, the 'Big Three' victors (United States, Soviet Union, United Kingdom) divided up many smaller countries and territories. In the case of North and South Korea, an arbitrary line was literally scratched across a map. Many of these ill-thought-out and nearly random divisions have been a source of friction ever since.

In 1947, British India was partitioned into India and Pakistan and to date there have been four 'official' wars, one undeclared war and endless border skirmishes. The first battles began in 1947 and ended in 1948, and were collectively known either as the First Indo-Pakistani War or the First Kashmir War. The largest of these conflicts were the Indo-Pakistani Wars of 1965 and 1971. In October 1962, India also fought a short, vicious and disastrous border conflict with communist China.

As with the Arab–Israeli Wars, massive mobile tank battles and air combat between modern jet aircraft dominated the headlines and garnered the most interest from other military forces. Still it was the infantry, as always, who had to be there to provide boots on the ground to end the conflicts. In 1965 and 1971, the Indian version of the FAL, the Ishapore-made 1A, equipped a great many of India's troops, although many were still armed with the Indian-built .303in No. 1 Mk III* Lee-Enfield in 1965. The 1A1, offering semi-automatic fire only, also saw service with the 1987 Indian Peace Keeping Force in Sri Lanka and most recently in the 1999 Kargil War.

The terrain itself in north-west India along the Pakistani border is infantry country, and light infantry country at that. Roads are few, logistics are a nightmare and the steep mountains make armoured or mechanized manoeuvres impossible. In October 1962, open fighting broke out between the People's Republic of China and India in a month-long war over the tense and disputed border along the Tibetan frontier. The Chinese Army soundly trounced the Indian Army in a series of actions despite some heroic last stands by Indian defenders. The Indian Army had rushed formations directly from low-altitude areas, clad in summer-issue clothing, armed with Lee-Enfields and often limited to the ammunition carried in their pouches, and the men suffered from the environment as much as the Chinese forces.

This debacle led to India raising its specialized mountain divisions, consisting of acclimatized local soldiers who were then well trained and equipped for combat in the Himalayan mountain ranges that line India's borders. These mountain divisions were high on the priority list to first receive the new 1A1 when it went into full production in 1963. Operating in rugged terrain with no armour, limited logistics trains and only some 75mm pack howitzers for indirect-fire support, the infantrymen in the mountain-warfare units found that their rifles took on considerably more significance. This fact had been noted in ski and mountain units since World War II: 'Fire fights of the infantry in snow-covered terrain take on added importance because the terrain can be kept under observation more easily and also because visibility is usually better. In cases where [mountain] troops have no artillery support, fire fights alone are frequently the only means of securing the success of the engagement' (MID 1942: 29).

Today, only India's Ishapore Arsenal, Brazil's IMBEL and De Santos Arms (DSA), based in Illinois, have the hardware to continue FAL production. While replaced in frontline Indian Army service by the 5.56×45mm INSAS assault rifle, some 1A1s still soldier on, in part because the newer INSAS, like the British SA80 and American M16, suffered considerable teething problems when first adopted. Mirroring the re-emergence of the American M14/M21, some scoped versions of the 1A1 are retained in frontline units to serve as DMRs to provide long-range precision firepower at the squad or section level.

The 1A1 rifle still sees use in the hands of some units in the contested high mountain border areas. India and Pakistan have skirmished for years in the mountains along the Line of Control (LOC) border in Kargil, including fighting on Siacham Glacier, the highest battlefield in the world at around 6,000m (c. 20,000ft) above sea level. Here, combat often comes down to small-unit scraps, squad on squad or even smaller, and the soldier's rifle remains crucially important.

In addition to Indian Army DMR use, reserve and non-military or semi-military forces have retained the 1A1. Special units such as the Sashastra Seema Bal (Armed Border Force), a paramilitary force of guards/trackers who police the remote mountain areas of the India–Nepal border, have kept their 1A1s, the longer range of the weapon and its dependability in cold and snow proving valuable in mountain warfare. Some Indian police forces also retain 1A1s; quite a few policemen brought their SLRs into play during the Mumbai terrorist attacks.

Private Bill Stallan of 6th Battalion, The Royal Australian Regiment on jungle patrol in Phuoc Tuy, 1971. Although the Australians' Lithgow-made L1A1s were supremely reliable and powerful, soldiers were initially only issued with five magazines, which they were expected to refill from bandoliers. (IWM MH 16767)

VIETNAM

Australian and New Zealand units fighting alongside US, South Vietnamese and other forces in Vietnam during the 1960s and 1970s were armed with the Lithgow-made L1A1 semi-automatic SLR; they found it a reliable weapon for jungle fighting. Despite very limited manpower and artillery and air support when compared to their American allies, the Australians and New Zealanders, by receiving special jungle training derived from lessons learned in the jungles of Malaya and Borneo, operated in a manner which the Viet Cong and NVA came to fear. Small Australian and New Zealand patrols moved like ghosts and often proved superior to the enemy when it came to stealth and fieldcraft. Despite the Australians' general disdain for the 'body count' as a measure of success, the statistics do provide considerable vindication of the unconventional methods they used.

Some estimates claim that American troops expended around 200,000 rounds of small-arms ammunition per enemy casualty; for the Australians and New Zealanders armed with the L1A1, 275 rounds were expended per enemy casualty (Hall & Ross 2009). The reasons for this were many. First, the Australian and New Zealand soldiers were trained to a standard of marksmanship far above and beyond that of the American infantryman. Second, many old hands in the 1st Australian Task Force were Borneo and Malaya veterans, reinforcing the jungle training Australian and New Zealand forces received before deployment to Vietnam. Third, the Australians and New Zealanders frequently operated in small, quiet, stealthy patrols rather than in huge, blundering, easily-avoided battalion-sized (or larger) sweeps.

Members of B Company of 2nd Battalion, The Royal Australian Regiment move with care after landing by helicopter, July 1967. The ANZACs in Vietnam often removed the carrying handles of their SLRs to save weight, and the flash hiders to cut length. (© Bettmann/Corbis)

The Australian method paid off in inflicting enemy casualties without the need for dozens of aircraft and thousands of artillery rounds per engagement. For instance, more than a third of the Australians' enemy contacts were ambushes. In 34 per cent of the cases, the Aussies and Kiwis ambushed the Viet Cong/North Vietnamese Army (VC/NVA) while in only 2 per cent of the contacts did the enemy manage to surprise the ANZACs in their own ambushes. One SAS study of Australian actions in Vietnam claimed that, despite the usually quite timely and relatively heavy air strikes and artillery support Western infantry enjoyed in that war, some 70 per cent of enemy casualties were inflicted with infantry small arms. The ANZACs' tactical methods also kept the enemy responding to them rather than vice versa, a critical element in counter-insurgency warfare.

Although its 1,143mm (45in) length was hardly ideal in the jungle, the SLR got very high marks for its ruggedness and dependability. The battle of Long Tan in August 1966 occurred in a pounding monsoon downpour and sloppy mud, conditions that caused more than a few problems for the M60 machine guns and their exposed ammunition belts, as well as the handful of the new American Armalite M16 rifles used by the Australians. The L1A1 weathered the test with flying colours; the official Australian Army after-action report called it 'the outstanding weapon of the action'. (Australian Army 1967: 26)

As with the British L1A1, the Australian SLR offered semi-automatic fire only. The conservation of ammunition provided by the semi-automatic made a real difference at Long Tan. Most soldiers were issued with, at best, one loaded magazine in the rifle and four spare magazines in their web gear; a total of 100 rounds or fewer does not last long in a set-piece long-term firefight, even on semi-automatic. Still, in the jungle, it was usually standard operating procedure to 'dump' the first magazine as fast as possible to establish fire superiority and then switch to the aimed 'double-tap' thereafter.

Even so, one of the biggest lessons of Long Tan was the issue of a great deal more ammunition and magazines to the infantryman. The issue of only five magazines, which were expected to be reloaded from bandoliers, was obviously insufficient for a soldier engaged in a firefight.

As with fighting men around the globe, the Australians and New Zealanders also quickly made use of the penetrative power of the 7.62×51mm NATO round. More than one enemy soldier hiding behind the trunk of a rubber tree found his cover turned into mere concealment by 7.62×51mm rounds blasting through it.

One semi-official modification of the L1A1 in Vietnam, which began in the Australian SAS, was nicknamed 'The Beast', or sometimes 'The Bitch'. This was an L1A1 converted to full-automatic fire with parts from the L2A1 SAW and the barrel, minus flash suppressor, cut off just beyond the gas-plug assembly. With a 30-round magazine, which it could empty in less than three seconds, it was a fearsome close-range weapon. More than a few soldiers of both sides thought the huge muzzle blast of 'The Beast' sounded like a heavy .50-calibre machine gun, providing a powerful psychological effect along with the extra firepower. Australian Recce veteran Peter Haran described his combat-zone modifications to his SLR:

> In Recce we had a choice of weapon, and I went back to the SLR [from the Armalite], but made a few adjustments. I replaced the safety catch with one from an L2A1 heavy-barrelled SLR and filed down the trigger sear and the pin designed to stop the safety catch from going 'auto'. With a 30-round instead of a 20-round magazine I now had the weapon I wanted in the bush – a 'Slaughtermatic', I called it: in essence a fully automatic 7.62mm machine gun without a belt-feed, a lightweight rifle with maximum punch when on automatic fire. I considered that too many magazines going through without a break were likely to melt the barrel, but if it ever came to that sort of fight I probably wouldn't be coming home anyway. (Haran & Kearney 2001: 32)

The FAL in Vietnam (opposite)

On 18 August 1966 at Long Tan, South Vietnam, elements of D Company, 6th Battalion, The Royal Australian Regiment made contact with what would turn out to be a regiment of Viet Cong supported by at least a battalion of North Vietnamese Army forces. The Australians were soon pinned down in a rubber plantation, just as the monsoon rains began to pour down. Despite the sea of mud and water, the Australians' L1A1 Self-Loading Rifles gave extremely reliable performance, the official after-action report calling the SLR the 'outstanding weapon of the action'.

The soldier shown here changing magazines could not have done so often; the official basic load at the time was one 20-round magazine in the weapon and four spares, for a total of 100 rounds of ammunition. Empty magazines were supposed to be reloaded from bandoliers. This system, of course, proved inadequate for combat. Only a daring low-level resupply drop from a helicopter kept D Company from running out of ammunition entirely during the engagement. The company commander recommended eight magazines per man after this battle.

Although the Australian Army had adopted the heavy-barrelled L2A2 SAW version of the FAL and had begun to make very promising improvements to the weapon, the adoption of the belt-fed American M60 7.62mm NATO machine gun, seen here, led to the L2A2's demise.

The rifles that fought the Falklands War. Above is the British L1A1 SLR and below is an Argentine folding-stock 'Para' FN FAL. (Neil Grant)

THE FALKLANDS WAR

In the Falklands War of 1982 between Argentina and Britain, the terrain was such that long-range heavy-calibre infantry weapons came into their own. Barren and nearly devoid of vegetation, the islands were usually windswept and the open, featureless terrain (weather permitting) offered unlimited visibility but made range estimation difficult.

The Falklands War was odd in that both sides' infantry were equipped with the FAL. The Argentine model was a Metric-pattern FAL, licence-manufactured locally, with full-automatic capability. Some Army troops received folding-stock 'Para' models, but it was the Argentine Naval Marines, operating from armoured amphibious tracked vehicles, who had significant numbers of the 'Para' version. Heavy-barrelled FAP SAWs were also in widespread use by the Argentine infantry. The British forces had their L1A1 SLRs, offering semi-automatic fire only, and had long preferred the L4 Bren to the heavy-barrelled FAL. Both sides, however, used the same GPMG, the FN MAG.

While a general misperception has grown over the years that the Falklands War was a cakewalk for the British, the late Major-General Sir Jeremy Moore, the commander of the British land forces during the conflict, called it, 'a damn close run thing.' Being volunteers and belonging to more elite light-infantry units such as the Royal Marines, Paras and Gurkhas, the British forces were better trained, with long traditions and a strong *esprit de corps*, which made them generally more aggressive than their opponents. In contrast, the Argentine forces consisted for the most part of conscripts with only a year or so of military service; some reinforcements rushed in had completed only 45 days of training. When well trained and led, however, the Argentine soldier was as good a combatant as could be found anywhere. After the Battle of Two Sisters on 11/12 June 1982, a senior British NCO said, 'They were good steadfast troops. I rate them.' High praise indeed coming from a sergeant-major in the Royal Marines.

With some notable exceptions, much of the Argentine officer corps proved to be unprofessional, self-serving and sometimes even abusive towards their men. Proving the old adage that there are no bad soldiers, only bad officers, Argentine units under good leadership gave the British unexpectedly stubborn opposition, however.

While the British also used the single-shot throw-away 66mm Light Anti-Tank Weapon (LAW) rocket, in Argentine accounts of the 1982 conflict the use of the Energa rifle-launched grenade is mentioned on numerous occasions; the Energa's use was frequent if not always effective. An Argentine officer, 2nd Lieutenant La Madrid, recalled his use of one during the confused night fighting on Mount Tumbledown (13/14 June 1982):

> I went through another gap in the rocks and was surprised by three men speaking in English behind and above me and firing over the top of me. I could see them with my night binoculars; there were about twelve of them in all. I was anxious to get back to my platoon. I took a rifle grenade and fired at where I had seen the first three men. I heard it explode and some shouts and cries of pain, and the sound of someone falling down the rocks. (Quoted in Middlebrook 1990: 265)

While the British used the SUIT, the Argentines employed scope-sighted FALs, many of them having high-quality German Hensoldt Zf scopes, and they also produced a dedicated FAL dust-cover scope mount for them. This Argentine mount is very solid and holds the scope much lower to the bore than the German STANAG mount, making it easier for a rifleman or sniper to get a cheek weld with the stock. The Argentines also possessed some dedicated sniper rifles, such as the US Model 700 Remington with 3–9× Redfield scope, and the M21; these proved deadly in well-trained hands.

Royal Marines conduct weapons training with their L1A1s aboard a Royal Fleet Auxiliary vessel during the voyage to the South Atlantic. (IWM FKD 2200)

A British sniper who served in the Falklands recalled that in exasperation with his rusty L42 Enfield he threw it away, picked up an Argentine FAL and used it as an impromptu sniping rifle for the rest of the campaign. Although it had no scope he commented that the lack of one was no hindrance, as it 'worked just fine out to four or five hundred yards' and the British scopes had all fogged up anyway. (Pegler 2006: 289)

Some Argentine forces were also equipped with the American AN/PVS-4 night-vision scope, which could be mounted on the FAL among other weapons, such as the FN MAG GPMG. It was a second-generation night-vision device (NVD), giving the user a good viewing range of 400–600m (437–656yd), with a range-finding and BDC reticle calibrated for the 7.62mm NATO round. It weighed 1.8kg (4lb). Argentine snipers equipped with the PVS-4 proved particularly deadly in the numerous night battles that occurred in the Falklands, a relative handful of these sharpshooters inflicting casualties far out of proportion to their numbers.

In contrast, British forces had only the 'Starlight' AN/PVS-2 night scope, known as the Individual Weapon Sight (IWS), a first-generation NVD weighing 2.7kg (6lb) and with a range of only 300–400m (328–437yd). Still, they made good use of it mounted on the L1A1. In addition to sniping individuals, a shooter armed with night sights would fire tracers at a target he had identified to guide the fire of his mates.

Technology notwithstanding, night fighting remained a particularly bloody and brutal short-ranged kind of combat. Corporal Steven Newland of 42 Commando Royal Marines described in detail the confused night combat on Mount Harriet on 11/12 June 1982. Believing his troop was pinned down by a single sharpshooter, Newland and another Marine crawled up silently through a maze of boulders. Instead of a lone sniper, there were ten Argentine soldiers, including one armed with a GPMG. They were taking only occasional single shots at the British below to give the impression of a single shooter. They were apparently hoping to lure

British soldiers heavily laden with SLRs and gear wait to embark by helicopter. (IWM FKD 2124)

the Marines into an assault on what they would think was only a single sniper, at which time they could open up with the machine gun and all their rifles when their targets emerged into the open – a perfect ambush. At about the same time Newland discovered this, he also found himself all alone, having lost his companion somewhere along the way.

The corporal made one of those apparently crazy combat decisions in which sheer audacity can succeed; he would assault the Argentine position single-handedly. Newland described the action:

> Then having made up my mind I picked up my SLR, changed the magazine and put a fresh one on and slipped the safety catch. I then looped the pin of one grenade onto one finger of my left hand and did the same with another. I was ready. So I thought, 'Well, you've got to do something.' I pulled one grenade, *whack* – straight onto the machine gun. Pulled the other, *whack* – straight at the spics [*sic*; a derogatory term used by the British of their Argentine opponents]. I dodged back round the rock and heard the two bangs. As soon as they'd gone off I went in and anything that moved got three rounds. I don't know how many I shot, but they got a whole mag. I went back round the rock, changed the mag and I was about to go back and sort out anyone who was left … (Quoted in Arthur 1987: 350)

A Royal Marine with his L1A1 rifle in the Falklands. (IWM FKD 94)

Newland had to pull back momentarily as the British troops below fired two 66mm LAW rockets at the Argentine position, then went back in again:

I went up by a different route and as I rounded this rock, I saw one of the guys that I'd hit. I'd only got him in the shoulder but he'd gone down like the rest of them and in the dark I'd automatically thought he was dead. But he was far from that, because as I came back round the corner, he just squeezed off a burst from his automatic. He must've realized he was going to die unless he got me first. I felt the bullets go into both my legs. I thought, 'Shit, I'm hit.' I was so angry I fired fifteen rounds into his head. (Arthur 1987: 351)

Many commentators and observers lauded the extra 'firepower' the Argentine forces enjoyed in having FALs capable of full-automatic fire, but this feature, nearly uncontrollable, generated much more noise than hits. Attacking Two Sisters (11/12 June 1982), one company of Royal Marines from 45 Commando was pinned down for an hour by a massive volume of Argentine small-arms and mortar fire. Despite the swarms of bullets coming in their direction, the Marines found that the only casualties they suffered came from shrapnel from the mortar bursts. In the battle for Wireless Ridge (13–14 June 1982), it was noted that only one Para was actually killed by small-arms fire. The indiscriminate shrapnel from mortars and artillery fire inflicted the majority of casualties.

The 1/7th Gurkha Rifles arrived too late for the majority of the major land battles of the war, but their experiences mirrored those of the Royal Marines. All the Gurkhas' wounded were hit by indirect fire, and the lone Gurkha killed outright was the victim of a landmine. One Argentine soldier complained that he and his colleagues had been told they had stockpiled ammunition sufficient for three to four days' worth of battle, but that they had burned up practically all of it in two to three hours of actual combat (Middlebrook 1987: 255).

In a spirited counter-attack mounted by Argentina's 7th Infantry Regiment to push the British Paras back off Mount Tumbledown, Private Horacio Benitez was one of approximately 20 men who gained the summit. As a FAP-gunner, he fought bravely against the inevitable British counter-attack, but did not feel his extra firepower did much good: 'Sergeant

Vallejos told me to open fire with my FAP. I fired a magazine of twenty rounds; when I was replacing the magazine, it seemed to me that the British were laughing. I opened fire again. Then the British rushed at us. I fired another magazine and then got into some cover'. (Quoted in Middlebrook 1990: 148). The firefight raged on and Benitez soon ran out of ammunition for his select-fire weapon. While trying to scrounge magazines from the body of a nearby casualty, he was severely wounded when a British bullet penetrated his helmet, and knocked him out of the fight.

The one aspect in which the Argentines' full-automatic FALs did provide a decided edge was in use against British aircraft, particularly helicopters. On the very first day of the battle, a group of Argentines reported by a British pilot as 'About forty men, firing automatic rifles' (Arthur 1987: 73) did serious damage to the British helicopter force in remarkably short order. Dubbed the 'Fanning Head Mob' by the British, this was actually a small detachment known as 'Eagle Detachment' under the command of 1st Lieutenant Carlos Esteban. These were actually the only Argentine forces close enough to oppose the unexpected British amphibious landing at San Carlos (21–25 May 1982), but they were too few in number to offer real resistance. When the landings began, Esteban withdrew his small force out of the village of San Carlos and into the hills.

Argentine FAL rifles piled beside the road leading to the airfield at Port Stanley, after the Argentine surrender on 14 June 1982. (IWM FKD 366)

To the Argentines' amazement, British helicopters began flying over. The first, a Westland Sea King HC.4, passed by the Argentine infantry unscathed, but the Argentines were now alerted and had the range. The Sea King's escort, a Westland Gazelle AH.1, flew within 91m (300ft) of the Argentines. Eagle Detachment unleashed all the fire they could from their FALs and FAPs on full-automatic; the helicopter was hit numerous times, but the pilot successfully made a forced landing in the bay. As the crewmen, one already injured, swam from the Gazelle, some of Esteban's men opened fire on the men in the water, and continued to do so until the lieutenant stopped them; one of many regrettable incidents in that war, and one that caused great anger among the British force.

As Eagle Detachment climbed to higher ground, another Gazelle appeared. Esteban reported:

> The small one nearly came over us; it was only about thirty or forty metres away. We opened fire and it was hit at once. It crashed only ten metres from me. It didn't burn but was badly crushed. I could see that both of the crew had died at once. Then another Gazelle came in. We opened fire on that one, and it got out quickly. (Middlebrook 1990: 148)

Unknown to the Argentines, they had done far greater damage than merely scaring off the helicopter. The second Gazelle had sustained hits from at least 14 7.62×51mm rounds, one passing through the cockpit and another knocking one of the blades off the tail rotor. Only the extreme skill of the pilot enabled the heavily damaged chopper to limp back to and land on the Landing Ship Logistic *Sir Galahad*.

On the British end of things, small arms became part of their air-defence system in San Carlos Bay when surface-to-air missiles (SAMs) alone could not stop the aggressive Argentine air strikes. The Argentine jets came in low and fast, the terrain around the bay cluttering British radar. The warships of the Royal Navy were primarily armed with Sea Dart high-altitude SAMs; only a very few had low-level Sea Wolf SAMs. Ashore, the vaunted Rapier missile systems of the ground forces took considerable time to get up and running, components having suffered from poor handling and rough seas en route. The Shorts Blowpipe man-portable SAM was nearly useless: 'like trying to shoot pheasants with a drainpipe,' according to Brigadier Julian Thompson, the British land commander in the Falklands conflict.

So the guns were brought back. Some of the ships had their decks virtually lined with GPMGs on improvised anti-aircraft mounts. Marines and seamen even armed themselves with L1A1s, often equipped with 30-round L4 Bren magazines and doctored to fire on full-automatic. When within range, the ground troops also unleashed every weapon at their disposal at attacking Argentine jets. The background audio of film footage of the air strikes in 'Bomb Alley' sounds like popcorn from the continuous crackle of small-arms fire.

That small arms needed to be integrated into the air-defence system showed that the British had placed too much faith in high-technology missiles. Some US Army officers seemed fascinated by this use of infantry weapons in the age of modern technology and later studied these actions in detail:

> British troops were preparing to move out of the beachhead at San Carlos Bay when four Argentine jets flying at a low level appeared without warning and headed out over the water. Forces on the ground firing small arms and automatic weapons placed a 'curtain of lead' in front of the flight path of the aircraft. As the four aircraft exited from the area, pieces of the tail section from one of the Mirages began to fall off and smoke appeared to be coming from out of its side just before

it crashed ... The use of a higher proportion of tracer rounds can disturb an enemy pilot's concentration enough to cause him to miss the target or abort his attack plan. (Cozad 1988)

Royal Marines of 40 Commando raise the British flag on West Falkland after the Argentine surrender. (IWM FKD 435)

In terms of the ground fighting, the battle for the Falklands was an acid test of the debate about the value of aimed semi-auto fire versus full-auto fire, a debate conducted largely through the FAL. In 1983 – not long after their involvement in the Falklands – a company of 1st Battalion, 7th Duke of Edinburgh's Own Gurkha Rifles conducted joint training with US Army Rangers at Fort Lewis, Washington State. The Rangers were, of course, suitably impressed by the Gurkhas:

Unlike American forces, who believe in small-caliber, fast-shooting semi- or full-auto rifles, Gurkha riflemen carry British-made FN semiauto only rifles in 7.62mm NATO caliber. Their legendary steel-clad nerves, which according to numerous reports allow them to return slow fire even when being shot at by automatic weapons, account for their philosophy of 'one kill for one shot'. And that's how they're trained ... they make every shot count ... 'We find that the extra weight of the larger caliber doesn't matter with the Gurkhas, because they're so strong,' offered Palmer [Captain John Palmer, Officer Commanding C Company, 1/7th Gurkha Rifles]. 'But the increased range and killing power possible with the 7.62, plus the effectiveness of aimed fire, makes them a very deadly soldier in combat ...' (Zambone 1983: 68)

CENTRAL AND SOUTH AMERICA

In Cuba, the revolution to overthrow the regime of president turned dictator Fulgencio Batista y Zaldívar (1901–73) sputtered from 1953 to 1956 before breaking out into fully fledged guerrilla warfare against government forces. When the United States could no longer overlook Batista's excesses, his principal source of arms and ammunition dried up, and he turned to Europe and procured FALs and heavy-barrelled FAPs. Thus FAL variants appeared in the hands of both sides – but then so did just about every type of military firearm.

Guerrilla leader and future head of state Fidel Castro (1926–) himself was most noted for his use of a scoped bolt-action Winchester Model 70 sporting rifle in .30-06 calibre. Later, he acquired an FAL as his personal weapon. When he marched victoriously into Havana with his rebels in 1959, he was carrying an FN-made Venezuelan FAL in the unusual 7×49.15mm 'Liviano' calibre. Weapons in this calibre were later rebarrelled to 7.62×51mm NATO.

The FAL as a SAW

SAW stands for squad automatic weapon, essentially an LMG used to provide a base of fire to suppress the enemy while the riflemen in the squad or section manoeuvre on that enemy. Examples of earlier weapons serving in this role would include the US Browning Automatic Rifle (BAR) and the British and Commonwealth Bren LMG. The heavy-barrelled 50.41 FALO version of the FAL was used as a SAW, and the variants manufactured in Argentina and Brazil are known as the FAP.

The Canadian and Australian armies worked together on their version of the FAL SAW, known as the C2A1 by the former and the L2A1 by the latter. As a weight-saving measure, the C2A1/L2A1 featured a unique front handguard that folded down to do double duty as a bipod. Two steel bipod legs with steel shoes were covered on three sides with wooden heat guards; when folded up to the bottom of the barrel, these formed the forearm. One problem immediately comes to mind, though; the gunner, after firing support in the prone position, could rush to advance without folding the handguards first and receive severe burns to his hand.

The Australian L2A1

Calibre:	7.62×51mm NATO
Length:	1,137mm (44.75in)
Barrel length:	533mm (21in)
Magazine:	30-round detachable box
Weight of full magazine:	0.68kg (1.5lb)
Empty weapon weight:	5.7kg (12.5lb)
Loaded weapon weight:	6.8kg (15lb)
Sights:	Blade foresight; dial aperture rear sight; adjustable for 200–1,000m (219–1,094yd)
Sight radius:	534mm (21in)
Cyclic rate of fire:	675–750rds/min
Effective rate of fire:	75rds/min

While a 6.8kg (15lb) weight is not light to an infantryman humping it over hill and dale, the FALO's weight wasn't bad when compared to other SAW types. It weighed 2kg (4lb 6oz) less than the BAR, 3.4kg (7lb 8oz) less than the Bren and 3.18kg (7lb) less than the more recent FN Minimi, whose 5.56×45mm ammunition also lacks the range and hitting power of the FALO's 7.62×51mm NATO.

Even so, reviews of the FALO were mixed. One universal complaint was that the longer 30-round magazine interfered with use of the weapon when fired from the prone position. Neither Argentina nor Israel even bothered with the larger 30-round magazines and universally issued the standard 20-round magazine for their SAWs. Australia was later to do the same. According to the Australian Army manual, the L2A1 is capable of:

a. delivering a high rate of aimed fire in single shots, or bursts of automatic fire, at ranges up to 600m [656yd];
b. continuous fire, using mostly single shots and some bursts of two or three rounds of automatic fire; and
c. long bursts of up to 10 rounds for short periods.
(Australian Army 1983)

Therein lies the rub. The SAW versions of the FAL require a *well-trained* soldier who would fire *short* and *aimed* bursts.

Conscript troops trained to a superficial standard almost universally point the muzzle in the general direction of the enemy and dump the full magazine on full-automatic.

The standard Metric-pattern versions of the FALO proved to be more user-friendly than the Canadian and Australian versions. The Israeli *Makleon* had a standard handguard improved with a perforated metal sleeve around the heavy barrel, and a wooden handguard with a heat shield. The folding bipod was attached directly to the barrel, as with the Austrian StG 58.

Despite the extra-thick contour of the barrel, the FALO did indeed get very hot with any extended firing. Most machine guns fire from an open bolt; that is, when not actually shooting, the bolt locks to the rear, allowing air to circulate through the barrel. Firing from a closed bolt, the FALO did not have anywhere near the cooling effect of an open-bolt weapon. After sustained firing and barrel heating, 'cook-offs' were possible, the cartridge immediately firing as it was chambered into the red-hot barrel.

ABOVE An FN-made FALO heavy-barrelled SAW with folding bipod, a long flash suppressor, and an adjustable rear peep sight graduated to 600m. It has a plastic stock, a plastic hollow pistol grip and a hardwood handguard with deep grooves. (Photo courtesy of Rock Island Auction Company)

The X2F2A2

The Australians experienced numerous problems with the L2A1 SAW as it was originally made in the FAP pattern. These were endemic to the breed and included: uncontrollability in full-automatic fire; prolonged firing leading to overheating and cook-offs; the bipod tilting out from under the axis of the bore from the torque of firing; an awkward prone firing position with 30-round magazines; and problems with firing in an assault position. During combat, more than one soldier forgot to fold up the bipod legs to use as a heat shield and instead grabbed the bare, red-hot barrel.

A new, upgraded weapon known as the X2F2A2 Automatic Rifle was developed from existing L2A1s. Improvements included a new in-line SAW-type butt with a handhold for the non-firing hand and a rubber butt pad. The wooden bipod/handguard combination was replaced with a

more conventional adjustable and swivelling bipod mounted to the barrel, which had the added benefit of lowering the shooter's profile by some 76mm (3in). The 30-round magazine was done away with in favour of the standard 20-round magazine. The new handguard had inner and outer perforated metal casings around the barrel to aid cooling by both conduction and convection, with the outer sleeve protected by a bonded rubber grip. A bolt hold-open device was added to lock the bolt open after the last round fired; a feature common to Metric-pattern FALs.

These and other modifications greatly improved the handling and accuracy of the FAL SAW. Two- or three-round bursts were well centred and the spread was 300 per cent better grouped than the L2A1's, which also had inevitably strayed downwards and left from the torque imparted by full-automatic fire. The X2F2A2, in semi-automatic mode and with use of the bipod, was considered accurate enough to be used in a sniping role with the Canadian C1 Leitz telescopic sight mounted. Further improvements led to the culmination of the project in the Australian X3F2A2.

What potential the weapon might have had in battle remains unknown, however. Development was suspended and the project grudgingly dropped when Australian forces entered the Vietnam War and were equipped with the American 7.62×51mm M60 machine gun – a dubious decision considering the problems the M60 has suffered throughout its lifespan.

Evaluating the FAL as a SAW

Commonwealth troops who used both the FALO and the Bren gun almost universally preferred the latter. The FALO, however, usually got higher marks than the M60 machine gun from those who had fired both. It has been noted that the FALO tended to experience a failure to feed the third round in the magazine. Most shooters experienced in using the FALO claim these stoppages almost always occur with 30-round magazines, especially if they are dirty. One American gun writer tested the FALO against the US M14A1 in the 1980s. (The M14A1 was to have been the SAW version of the M14, and featured a folding bipod and foregrip to enable the firer to control recoil better.) Using 20-round magazines, he experienced only two malfunctions (one ammunition-related) while putting 2,500 rounds through the FALO.

In early 1959, only two months after taking power, Castro sent a Major Ricardo Lorie to Belgium to purchase some US $9 million-worth of arms for the new regime directly from FN. The arms included some 22,500 FALs, 50 million rounds of 7.62mm ammunition and compatible rifle grenades. An unknown number of heavy-barrelled FAPs also found their way into Cuban service. The FALs delivered from FN were stamped with the Cuban Coat of Arms as used on the FALs purchased earlier by Batista. These crests supposedly enraged Castro. When the Soviets helped equip the Cuban military with AK-47s, the FALs were mothballed, but many found their way to Venezuela, El Salvador, Chile and Nicaragua in the hands of Cuban 'advisors' supporting insurgents in those nations. In the early 1980s, an 'unknown' FAL variant showed up in the hands of communist guerrillas in El Salvador; these were notable for a hole the size of a quarter (24mm) cut through the magazine well in the upper receiver. It turned out that these mystery FALs were Cuban weapons which had had the coat of arms removed.

The FN FAL was and remains popular throughout much of the Americas. These FAL-armed troops are from the Eastern Caribbean Defence Force, a coalition of Caribbean nations that supported the US-led invasion of Grenada in 1983. (DoD)

The FAL was – and in some cases remains – extremely popular throughout South and Central America, not least in the high Andes during the Cenepa War, the short-lived border dispute between Ecuador and Peru in January and February 1995, the climax of decades of skirmishing over the line. Both Argentina and Brazil manufactured their own versions of the FAL and FAP as well as exporting their weapons to Paraguay, Peru, Chile, Ecuador and Bolivia. These weapons continue to be used in government clashes with bandits, insurgents, smugglers and drug cartels.

Brazil in particular, although possessing modern conventional military forces, has to police the endless rainforests of the vast Amazon Basin – strictly light-infantry country. The Army includes no fewer than five specially trained and equipped Jungle Infantry Brigades, and has a renowned Jungle Warfare Instruction Centre at which US Special Forces (Green Berets), British SAS soldiers and Légionnaires of France's Légion Étranger (Foreign Legion) have attended training for jungle warfare.

The locally manufactured IMBEL FAL in its various makes and models, especially 'Para' and carbine versions, remains in frontline service with some Brazilian forces. Brazil is retooling its FAL production lines to begin refurbishing – and resume the manufacture of – the FAL. There is even talk of Brazil's armed forces retaining the 7.62×51mm NATO as a standard rifle calibre and not switching over fully to the 5.56×45mm.

IMPACT
The quintessential battle rifle

What was the FAL's great impact on military operations? It was intended to equip NATO infantry to face down hordes of Soviet tanks and mechanized infantry swarming into Central Europe in a Third World War. Thankfully, the FAL never had to fulfil this particular purpose.

It was introduced at a time when the face of war was changing from major set-piece conventional warfare, as in World War II, to insurgencies and revolutions; so-called 'small wars'. It served very well in these 'brushfire wars', and was many an infantryman's best friend. For the most part, it set the standard for a reliable, sturdy and accurate military weapon for professional soldier and conscript alike. To many, it remains the quintessential battle rifle.

The FAL/SLR has many strengths that endear it to users to this day. The main point most often mentioned is the sheer power of the 7.62×51mm NATO cartridge – no matter how it came about.

THE 7.62×51mm NATO

Regardless of the political activity that went on before its adoption, and the tantalizing speculation about the .280in/7mm round over which it triumphed, the 7.62×51mm NATO did turn out to be an excellent, powerful military cartridge. It was used in a variety of weapons that gave sterling service around the world and continue in use to this day. With millions of FALs manufactured and internationally distributed, the rifle played a large part in making the 7.62×51mm NATO the success it was. Just as the FAL is often regarded as the quintessential post-war battle rifle, the 7.62mm NATO is regarded as the consummate battle-rifle calibre.

Penetration

When it comes to performance, even the standard M80 147-grain full metal jacket (FMJ) round in 7.62mm offers substantial penetrative power, even though it is a first-generation bullet designed in 1953 with a soft-lead core under a light gliding metal jacket. It can penetrate a 3.45mm (0.14in) standard NATO steel plate at 620m (678yd), which is also listed as its maximum effective range. Chambered in a variety of sniper rifles, it has been used quite successfully to ranges of 1,000m (1,094yd) and even a bit beyond. Although packing more recoil than the intermediate rounds, the 7.62mm round's power and range endeared it to many of its users.

Long after other forces had gone over fully to the 5.56mm assault rifles, some specialized units continued to use the 7.62mm battle rifle. For instance, for use in mountain environments troops such as the German Gebirgsjäger retained the 7.62mm G3 and the Italian Alpini their BM-59 after the regular infantry of these two nations had gone over to the 5.56mm G36 and M70 Beretta respectively. Austria's elite forces, the Jagdkommando, kept the StG 58 until the mid-1990s; as they had trained to operate behind enemy lines in case of a Soviet invasion, they wanted a rifle that could outrange the enemy's Kalashnikovs and deal heavier and more destructive blows against soft-skinned rear-echelon vehicles.

In urban environments the superior penetration offered by the 7.62×51mm round has gained new appreciation after infantry experiences in places like Mogadishu, Baghdad, Fallujah and Kabul over the last two decades. A comparison between the 7.62×51mm NATO M80 Ball and the 5.56×45mm M193 55-grain ball that replaced it shows why.

In military parlance, the 7.62×51mm round 'turns cover into concealment'. There are certain situations, however, in which the 7.62×51mm delivers too much power. In British Guiana (since 1966 the independent country of Guyana) in 1963, where British troops had been deployed since the previous year to quell civil unrest, a small patrol of 1st Battalion, The Coldstream Guards, was surrounded by a mob of rioters who refused to disperse. A single round was fired from an SLR; that one bullet killed three people and wounded another (Dewar 1984: 65). In military use, of course, ammunition besides FMJ was developed, such as tracer, armour-piercing and other specialized rounds.

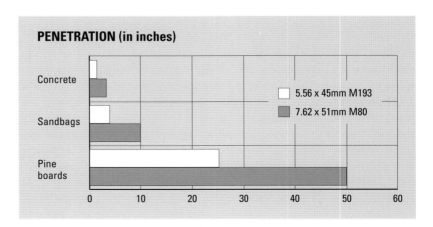

Range

With the additional power of the 7.62×51mm NATO in the FAL/SLR comes longer range, especially for the soldier sufficiently trained in marksmanship to utilize that benefit. In mountainous areas such as Afghanistan, and in open spaces like the Falklands, the desert and the Arctic, range is king. A 2009 British MoD study stated that well over half of the British forces' firefights in Afghanistan occurred at ranges of between 300m and 900m (328 and 984yd; Drummond & Williams 2009: 9). An American source in Helmand stated the average engagement range encountered was 500m (547yd; Wall 2010: 2). Here the value of the 7.62×51mm round quickly became apparent, and 7.62mm NATO weapons were reissued down to squad or section level, although the FAL/SLR was not among those weapons. The assault-rifle theory that the average engagement range need not exceed 300m (328yd) applies in most environments, but not all.

While the FAL's effective range is listed as 600m (656yd) and the sights were graduated to that range, it is certainly capable of inflicting casualties out to 800m (875yd) in good hands. With the 4× L2A2 SUIT or the 4× Hensoldt Zf 24, first-shot hits on man-sized silhouette targets out to 600m (656yd) are feasible. Beyond that range one requires 'sighting shots' to 'walk' the bullet impacts onto the target to determine the proper hold-over and hold-off – that is, moving the sight or reticle off the target itself to compensate for wind drift or ranges further than the sight is designed for.

In the 1980s Belgium adopted the FNC assault rifle as its 5.56mm replacement for the venerable FAL. It has been made under licence, with adaptations, in Indonesia (as the Pindad SS1) and Sweden (as the Ak 5) and sold to several other nations. (Rama/CC-BY-SA-2.0-FR)

THE FAL'S REPUTATION

With the exception of the Israeli experience, the FN FAL set the West's standard for durability, ruggedness and reliability. Apart from its weight, the above attributes led many veterans who used the FAL/SLR to retain a fondness and even affection for the old warhorse; American veterans of wars past often have a similar enduring nostalgia for the M1 Garand. Soldiers, Marines and airmen from military forces around the world recall their FALs with much fondness. The author certainly does not remember the M16A1 with anything even approaching affection.

Reliability

As noted earlier, the FAL/SLR served from the Canadian Arctic to the Falklands, in jungle and desert, and in many hostile urban environments.

While good troops always observe proper cleaning and maintenance of their weapons, sometimes it is just not possible to keep them spotless at all times. How well does the FAL stand up when subjected to real use and abuse above and beyond the call of duty?

In 2001, a group of American gun writers gave a DSA-manufactured SA58 standard FAL a torture test that involved firing 10,000 rounds of ammunition over a period of nine hours. When the rifle became too hot to hold, it was cooled off in a snowbank. When a pin sheared on the forearm, it was fixed with a bent nail. When a Steyr gas plug failed, it was replaced in three minutes with a DSA-made part. And they kept firing. The barrel was of course completely shot out by the end of the ordeal, but headspace had increased only 0.025mm (0.001in) and the gun was still firing and still able to put its shots into a man-sized silhouette at a range of 91m (100yd). This torture test ended not when the SA58 FAL gave up, but when the testers ran out of ammunition! (Fortier 2002: 36–42)

COMPARISONS

It is instructive to compare the FAL to its main rivals in the realm of battle rifles, namely the M14 and the G3.

M14

Although used by only a tiny handful of nations compared to the other battle rifles, the M14 was certainly a fine battle rifle. Just like the FAL and the G3, however, the 7.62×51mm cartridge keeps it from being controllable in full-automatic fire. In fact, the full-automatic feature was disabled on the vast majority of M14s. A gas-operated weapon with a 20-round detachable magazine, the M14 can be seen as an improved and modernized version of the M1 Garand of World War II fame – which, while not a bad thing, still begins with late 1930s technology.

The M14 is the lightest of the three battle rifles by roughly 0.45kg (1lb), lightness always being appreciated by the infantryman. The main combat service of the M14 was during the early phases of American involvement in the Vietnam War. The M14 is nearly always more accurate than the FAL, due to both design and its excellent sights. In fact, the M14 saw much longer service as the M21 sniper rifle version than it did as a battle rifle. Upgraded M14s are still in service with US forces around the world.

G3

The Heckler & Koch G3 traced an interesting path. It was originally based on a prototype Mauser design at the end of World War II, which was further developed in post-war Spain as the Model 58 series of CETME rifles. After the disagreement over FN allowing Germany to manufacture FALs, the Germans took another look at the CETME design and eventually Heckler & Koch was to hone the design in 7.62×51mm NATO as the G3 (*Gewehr* 3).

The G3 is the heaviest of the three battle rifles, although weighing only slightly more than the FAL. It utilizes a unique roller locking system, and all in all, the G3 may well be the most rugged modern military rifle ever made. The G3 suffers from two major flaws from the standpoint of the user, however.

First, the trigger is almost universally atrocious; I have found this to be the case with G3s, HK91s and CETMEs. A bad trigger is perhaps the greatest obstacle to good marksmanship. Second, the G3 lacks a mechanism to lock the bolt to the rear after the last round in the magazine has been fired. Many a soldier has pulled the trigger on an empty chamber with this system. Inherently, the G3 is capable of great accuracy. Practically, its poor trigger and sights provide less field accuracy than the other battle rifles. As with the others, calibre also keeps it from being a true assault rifle.

After the FN FAL, the Heckler & Koch G3 is the second most popular battle rifle of the post-war era. With a roller-delayed blowback action, it is perhaps even more rugged than the FAL, though let down by its poor trigger. This Marine was photographed testing a G3 in Manda Bay, Kenya, 2003. (US Marine Corps)

Comparative specifications – FN FAL, H&K G3, M14

	FN FAL	H&K G3	M14
Calibre	7.62×51mm NATO	7.62×51mm NATO	7.62×51mm NATO
Weight	4.31kg (9lb 8oz)	4.4kg (9lb 11oz)	3.88kg (8lb 9oz)
Length	1,053mm (41.5in)	1,025mm (40.4in)	1,117mm (44in)
Barrel length	533mm (21in)	450mm (17.7in)	558mm (22in)
Magazine	20-round detachable box	20-round detachable box	20-round detachable box
Cyclic rate of fire	650–700rds/min	500–600rds/min	750rds/min
Muzzle velocity	853m/sec (2,800ft/sec)	780–800m/sec (2,560–2,625ft/sec)	853m/sec (2,800ft/sec)

THE FAL'S WEAKNESSES

Weight

The FAL certainly had its weaknesses, mainly weight and length. British and Australian rifle manuals even included special strengthening exercises for those who would wield the SLR. Weight does not endear any weapon to the infantryman. In addition to the weight of the weapon, the soldier has to carry the ammunition for it. Here was the greatest argument in favour of the 5.56×45mm NATO cartridge when it replaced the 7.62×51mm round. With lighter ammunition, the soldier could carry more of it. In an age when the concept of volume of fire and suppressive fire was taking over military thinking, a soldier carrying more cartridges was a major selling point.

A single round of 7.62mm ammunition (M80) weighs 25.40g (392 grains), while a single 5.45×45mm SS109 cartridge weighs only 12.31g (190 grains) – a weight reduction of approximately half. To the cartridge weight must be added the weight of the magazine; a seemingly insignificant difference, but not when multiplied by six or eight of them in the infantryman's magazine pouches. A full 20-round (steel) magazine of 7.62×51mm ball ammunition weighs 730g (1lb 12oz) compared to 459g (1lb) for a 30-round aluminium magazine of 5.56mm ball.

A comparison of Cold War rifles. From top to bottom: the American 7.62mm M14; German 7.62mm H&K G3; American 5.56mm AR-15 (which became the M16); French 7.5mm MAS 49/56; 7.62mm FN FAL. (Neil Grant)

Length

Length was another major Achilles heel of the FAL, especially with the SLR's 1,143mm (45in) length being slightly longer than the .303in Lee-Enfield No. 4 rifle it replaced!

In urban fighting, such length cost the soldier valuable time and manoeuvrability in the tight spaces characteristic of house-to-house street fighting, and it was less than ideal in thick jungle growth. A paratrooper exiting an aircraft or an air-assault infantryman leaping from a helicopter does not appreciate excess weapon length, either. It should go without saying that mechanized/armoured infantry exiting hatches on APCs or IFVs find a shorter rifle desirable as well. In fact, a former British soldier serving with the British Army of the Rhine, whom I met in Germany during the Cold War, was less impressed with his L1A1 than I was; riding in the low-profile FV432 APC, he claimed 'SLR' actually stood for 'Stupidly Long Rifle'.

The FAL's length was not inevitable, but once more we are playing the 'what if?' game regarding the .280in intermediate calibre. An early FAL prototype, the FN No. 2 'short' carbine, was a bullpup design intended to compete with the EM-2; despite having a 585mm (23in) barrel, it was only 860mm (33.9in) long. Other early FN FAL prototypes, both light- and heavy-barrelled models, had 482mm (19in) barrels rather than the 533mm (21in) barrels that became military standard.

The FAL eventually evolved by increments to combat the problems of length and weight, incorporating shorter barrels, lightweight aluminium lower receivers and folding stocks. For the SLR, a 457mm (18in) or 482mm (19in) barrel and a shorter muzzle device, such as the Belgian-pattern short flash hider, could have saved the infantryman 152mm (6in) or so of length.

Today, the latest rage among commercially produced FALs is the carbine with 412.75mm (16.25in) barrel, which in the standard fixed-stock version is 952.5mm (37.5in) long overall and weighs 3.78kg (8lb 5oz) empty and without accessories (sling, magazine, etc.). An SA58 FAL 'Para' with the same barrel length folds down to 724mm (28.5in) and weighs a manageable 3.8kg (8lb 6oz).

Still, as we all know, no matter the rifle or the modifications, the 'perfect' rifle does not and will no doubt never exist. The best that can be hoped for is a rifle that does most things well. The argument over the 'best' rifle is one that will probably never end.

The great debate: firepower versus accuracy

Advocates of the larger-calibre main battle rifles almost universally argue that steel on target – i.e. accuracy – is what constitutes real firepower. On the other hand, real select-fire assault rifles and modern military doctrine call for firepower via volume of fire. This disagreement still rages on between the various adherents and will no doubt go on for decades to come.

As renowned military historian the late John Keegan saw it, '"Wasting ammunition", for decades the cardinal military sin, has in consequence become a military virtue; "hitting the target", for centuries the principal military skill, is henceforth to be left to the law of averages'. (Keegan 1978: 262). American military historian Brigadier General S.L.A. Marshall's observations that during the Korean War small-arms engagements were conducted at short ranges (within 229m/250yd) added weight to the World War II statistics the Germans used to determine the need for an assault rifle effective only to 300m (328yd). These observations served to amplify the demand for full-automatic assault rifles in the hands of every infantryman. Often overlooked, though, is the fact that Marshall argued repeatedly that full-automatic assault rifles were not a good idea: 'Suffice to say now that any trend toward eliminating the semi-automatic, hand-carried weapons in favor of full-automatic weapons in the hands of all infantrymen should be vigorously combated' (Marshall 1958).

During the night-long attacks made by Chinese forces against US infantry positions in Korea, Marshall noted that on more than one occasion all of the American automatic weapons (LMG, BAR, M2 carbine, submachine gun) had run completely dry while the riflemen armed with the semi-automatic M1 Garand always had ammunition left – enough to settle the issue during the last desperate hours or even minutes of combat when both sides were on their last legs.

CONCLUSION

The FAL still appears in military and law-enforcement use, most recently showing up in the Libyan Civil War. In a few countries, FALs remain in active-duty service, while other nations retain FALs for use by reserve forces or as basic trainee weapons. Civilian contractors in the world's war zones, able to choose their own weapons, sometimes pick the FAL. UN peacekeepers are sometimes still armed with versions of the FAL.

In South America in particular, the FAL stubbornly hangs on in military service. Argentina and Brazil have held onto most of their FALs. Argentina is, in fact, currently rebuilding some 100,000 of its old FALs, and experimenting with new and improved versions. At one end of the spectrum, units which engage in jungle and urban fighting have short-barrelled FAL carbines; at the other end, FALs have been fine-tuned into long-range precision sniper rifles. Argentina has plans to retool one of the DGFM arms plants to resume production of various versions of the FAL. Neither do the Argentines have plans to change over to the 5.56×45mm round. Keeping in mind some of the serious performance issues of that calibre, as seen in recent and ongoing conflicts, perhaps this is not a bad idea. Argentina will also be building 'accurized' Match-grade models of the FAL for use as scoped semi-automatic sniper rifles, known as the Rifle, Semiautomatic, Precision.

The 7.62×51mm NATO round's combination of range and stopping power has led the Indian Army to fit scopes to versions of their 1A1 for use as a DMR. Although regular Indian Army units now have the 5.56×45mm INSAS or Israeli 5.56×45mm Tavor TAR-21 rifles, those reserve and paramilitary units tasked with patrolling the vast mountain wilderness along India's borders with China and Pakistan retain the 1A1, as do many police forces.

Today's civilian shooters – especially in the United States – have a real affinity with the FAL, which keeps commercial manufacture and sales going

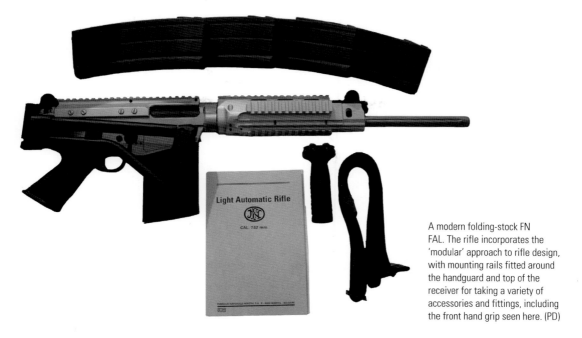

A modern folding-stock FN FAL. The rifle incorporates the 'modular' approach to rifle design, with mounting rails fitted around the handguard and top of the receiver for taking a variety of accessories and fittings, including the front hand grip seen here. (PD)

strong. DSA Inc. of Illinois is the leading manufacturer of American FALs and continues to produce all-new weapons. In addition to the standard rifle, carbine and 'Para' models, one interesting weapon intended for use by military and police is the SA58 OSW (Objective Sniper Weapon), available in semi-automatic-only or select-fire versions. The OSW has barrels as short as 330mm (13in) or even 279mm (11in); the latter version is only 590.5mm (23.25in) overall long with the stock folded. At the other end of the DSA spectrum is the SA58 SPR, a rugged sniper rifle comparable to the Argentine precision semi-automatic rifle. The spate of urban battlefields this century has led to requests for larger-capacity semi-automatic rather than bolt-action sniper rifles, and the SPR was actually submitted to the US Army for its SASS Rifle Trials. Examples have also been spotted in the hands of New Zealand and Australian SAS troopers deployed to Afghanistan.

In between these two, a wide variety of semi-automatic choices for the civilian shooter is available, from the standard fixed-stock FAL to a 'Para' folding-stock model with a 413mm (16.26in) barrel. For hunters, some of the rifles are also chambered for .243 Winchester and .260 Remington hunting cartridges. Despite all the different outward appearances, they are all FALs at heart.

As much as some would like it, the FN FAL is not going to be brought back as a service rifle in the West. One always has to wonder what would have happened had the .280in British round been adopted instead of the 7.62×51mm round. Perhaps, like the venerable Soviet 7.62×39mm round, it would still be in use as a standard calibre. With the .280in round, the FAL, with various improvements over the years, no doubt would have also enjoyed a much longer service life, as have the various Kalashnikovs. Hypothetical questions aside, historically the FAL/SLR did indeed serve long and well with more than 90 countries and has more than earned its moniker of 'the Right Arm of the Free World'.

BIBLIOGRAPHY

Secondary sources

Arnold, Dave (1987). 'Fabrique Nationale's World-Class Battle Rifles', Assault Firearms (*Guns & Ammo*), Vol. 5, No. 1: 66.

Arthur, Max (1987). *Above All, Courage*. London: Sphere Books.

Cozad, Andrea (1988). *Light Infantry in Action*. Newsletter 1-88. Fort Leavenworth, KS: Center for Army Lessons Learned.

Dewar, Michael (1984). *Brush Fire Wars: Minor Campaigns of the British Army since 1945*. London: Robert Hale.

Dodd, Colonel Norman L. (1976). 'The Corporal's War: Internal Security Operations in Northern Ireland', *Military Review*, July 1976, 58.

Fortier, David (2001). 'Austria's FAL; The StG58', *Shotgun News*, 20 January 2001, 23.

Fortier, David M. (2002). 'Nine-hour 10,000-round DSA Torture Test', *Guns Magazine*, August 2002, 36–42

Geraghty, Tony (1982). *Inside the SAS*. New York, NY: Ballantine.

Hall, Bob & Ross, Andrew (2009). 'Bang on Target? Infantry Marksmanship and Combat Effectiveness in Vietnam', *Australian Army Journal*, Volume VI, Number 1, Autumn 2009, 139–53.

Haran, Peter & Kearney, Robert (2001). *Crossfire: An Australian Reconnaissance Unit in Vietnam*. Sydney: New Holland.

Hoare, Major Michael (2008). *The Road To Kalamata: A Congo Mercenary's Personal Memoir*. Boulder, CO: Paladin Press.

Keegan, John (1978). *The Face of Battle*. New York, NY: Penguin Books.

Luttwak, Edward & Horowitz, Dan (1975). *The Israeli Army*. New York, NY: Harper & Row.

Marshall, Brigadier General S.L.A. (1958). *Sinai Victory: Command Decisions in History's Shortest War, Israel's 100-Hour Conquest of Egypt East of Suez*. Nashville, TN: Battery Press.

Middlebrook, Martin (1990). *The Fight for the Malvinas*. New York, NY: Penguin.

Pegler, Martin (2006). *Out of Nowhere: A History of the Military Sniper*. Oxford: Osprey Publishing

Rabinovich, Abraham (2004). *The Yom Kippur War: The Epic Encounter that Transformed the Middle East*. New York, NY: Shocken Books

Rose, Alexander (2008). *American Rifle: A Biography*. New York, NY: Delacorte Press.

Stevens, Blake (1982). *The FAL Rifle: Volume One*. Toronto: Collector Grade Publications.

Wall, Jeffrey (2010). 'A Rifleman's War', *Small Wars Journal*, October 2010, 2.

Weller, Jac (1966). 'British Weapons and Tactics in Malaysia', *Military Review*, November 1966, 17.

Weller, Jac (1973). 'Israeli Paratroopers', *Military Review*, March 1973, 49.

Zambone, Joe (1983). 'Gurkhas Under Fire: the Business of Blood 'n' Guts', *Eagle Magazine*, August 1983.

Official publications

Australian Army (January 1967). *HQ, 1 Australian Task Force, Commanding Officer After Action Report,* Operation Smithfield, 1-31.

Australian Army (1983). *Infantry Training Volume 4 Pamphlet No 5 The Self-Loading Rifle, 7.62 mm L1A1 and Automatic Rifle, 7.62 mm L2A2.* Training Command.

British Army (1950). *Provisional Notes for Users of Rifle, Automatic, .280-IN, E.M. 1.* London: HMSO.

British Army (1958). *The Conduct of Anti-Terrorist Operations in Malaya.* 3rd Edition. Far East Land Forces Command.

Military Intelligence Division, US Army (1942). *German Ski Training and Tactics.* Washington, DC: War Department.

Ministry of Defence, UK (1975). *User Manual for Sight Unit Infantry Trilux.*

Rhodesian Security Forces (1971). *Anti-Terrorist Operations Manual.*

Other sources

http://www.arrse.co.uk/weapons-equipment-rations/186362-why-did-they-replace-slr-19.html/

http://www.israelmilitary.net/showthread.php?t=12379&highlight=rifle/

Bennett, Bob, interview. *SAS Heroes: Last Stand in* Oman. Fivetv, documentary, 2008.

Biswas, Kunal. Email to author. 20/03/2012.

Creamer, Steve. Email to author. 20/05/2012.

Drummond, Nicholas & Williams, Anthony G. (2009). *Biting the Bullet.* (http://www.quarry.nildram.co.uk/btb.pdf/)

Farrar, Paul (COL). Email to author. 08/04/2012.

Love, John. 'Missing, Presumed P***ed'. Britain's Small Wars website (www.britains-smallwars.com/Falklands, quoted with permission).

Rhodes, Ian. *Rhodesian Cover Shooting* (http://feraljundi.com/tag/rhodesian-cover-shooting, quoted with permission).

INDEX